PRAISE FOR
REDEMPTIVE LEADERSHIP

We are living in a day of leadership madness where character has been exchanged for confidence and integrity jettisoned for results. We are more desperate today for good leaders and meaningful material on leadership than ever before. Harv Powers offers a lucid and deep understanding of the developmental journey a leader must walk to offer not only vision but life. Harv is a brilliant, tender, and wise man whose labor will reinvigorate your leadership and clarify your next steps in your calling.

— Dan B. Allender, founding president and professor of counseling psychology at the Seattle School of Theology and Psychology and author of The Wounded Heart and Leading with a Limp

If you have experienced a crisis as a leader—and who hasn't?—Dr. Harv Powers's book Redemptive Leadership is for you. The wisdom he has gathered through coaching, mentoring, and studying great leaders will change the way we think about the role of crisis as a key catalyst in the internal development of leaders, a topic seldom discussed in current leadership literature. In his view, this internal growth supports longevity as a leader and spawns what he defines as redemptive influence. Don't miss out on this important leadership discussion as it will change how we understand what truly shapes the internal life of a leader.

— *Curt Coffman, senior partner at the Coffman Organization, executive fellow at Daniels School of Business, and coauthor of First, Break All the Rules*

Harv Powers takes leadership development to a whole new level—beyond just understanding and applying methods and principles which increase competency. He shows how God transforms leaders' lives by using failure and brokenness to cause growth in effectiveness and usefulness. I have taught leadership development for almost fifty years and believe what Dr. Powers shares in this book will be important additions to what I teach in the future.

— *Steve Douglass, president of Campus Crusade for Christ International and Cru and coauthor of Managing Yourself and How to Achieve Your Potential and Enjoy Life*

Emerging from his many years of caring for Christian leaders, Dr. Powers weaves together biblical wisdom, life experiences, and professional expertise to provide insight into how God develops, restores, and matures us as members of His leadership team. Redemptive Leadership will show you how you can embrace God's leadership development path and find greater hope, joy, and eternal effectiveness.

— Craig Williford, president and associate professor of leadership at Multnomah University

This leadership book is a refreshing departure from the standard shallow professional advice I read so often. Harv Powers is onto something fresh with his five-stage Redemptive Leadership Model. I agree with him that the best leadership often springs from the ashes. God uses us because of our brokenness, not in spite of our brokenness. This book is a great culmination of Dr. Powers's decades of helping hurting leaders.

— Hans Finzel, president of HDLeaders and best-selling author of The Top Ten Mistakes Leaders Make

Dr. Harvey Powers, a skilled and sought-after therapist and speaker, draws from his deep experience as a pastor and counselor in this valuable book, which will enlighten leaders and followers alike to the meaning of godly influence. There is much more to leadership than "the gospel of knowledge and duty," as Dr. Powers points out. In Scripture and in our lives today, we find that God sculpts us through crisis and failure, which are integral parts of the journey toward personal transformation. Indeed, Dr. Powers has helped me greatly through my own dark nights of the soul. May God use this short, but profound, book to bring beauty out of ashes and to bring many Christians to a better understanding of God's narrative for their lives.

— *Douglas Groothuis, professor of philosophy at Denver Seminary and author of thirteen books, including Walking through Twilight*

In these current days where we question leadership in every sphere of influence, Dr. Powers gives powerful insight into the experiences and qualities that make for a true leader. This is the book that anyone interested in leadership development should read to understand what it takes to build authentic leaders.

— Nanci Ricks, president of Empart USA

Books on leadership abound (and Harv Powers cites many of them), but this book stands out from the pack. While acknowledging the importance of competency, work ethic, intelligence, character, and other crucial traits of successful leaders, Dr. Powers draws readers into the transforming power of redemptive experiences. Using many illustrations—from his own thirty-plus years of experience as well as biblical examples—he charts a course for emerging, experienced, and re-emerging leaders to redeem their own brokenness (and no leader is exempt) to become agents of redemption in the lives of others—which becomes Powers' definition of a truly successful leader. His key takeaway: "God uses us because of our brokenness, not in spite of our brokenness."

— William W. Klein, professor of New Testament at Denver Seminary and author of The New Chosen People

Many leaders and their organizations dangle on the precipice of disaster. This is not because we don't have enough leadership knowledge, but something far more personal. Dr. Powers offers a powerful lifeline to the individual who is gifted to lead but is experiencing a disconnect between personal character and leadership influence. This book gives a transformational pathway to more effective and fulfilling leadership both professionally and organizationally.

— Joe Henseler, lead pastor at
Faith Church, Allentown, PA

When I was officially recognized and appointed as a church leader, it was exhilarating. Soon after the appointment, I recognized that my background and personal brokenness made me feel unworthy. Learning the Redemptive Leadership Model, as described in this book by Dr. Powers, helped me to move from my doing and hiding to my being and sharing God's redemption in my life. This Redemptive Leadership Model has the power to set leaders free.

— Minner Labrador, president of Upper Columbia
Conference, Seventh-Day Adventist Church

Harvey Powers gives us hope by showing us how brokenness is different from woundedness. Woundedness breeds defensiveness while brokenness releases life. Powers doesn't just show us the city on the hill but gives us a road map on how to get there. I know—he did for me, and my journey has been sweeter because I have a redemptive story to tell. Get this book if you are serious about being the leader God can use to bring redemption to others.

— Rodney L. Cooper, Kenneth and Jean Hansen Chair of Discipleship and Leadership at Gordon-Conwell Theological Seminary

Real-life stories liberally illustrate the pages, and biblical reflections saturate the text. All this makes it easy to read. However, don't be misled into thinking it is simplistic because the five-stage model of Redemptive Leadership is profound and the invitation to take the journey towards growth and transformation is challenging indeed.

— Bill Houston, scholar care giver at the John Stott Ministry, South Africa

Organizations around the world need redemptive leaders that will provide healing, forgiveness, and hope for the future in the dark moments of the lives of leaders and those they lead. Dr. Harvey Powers has written a book for which I have been waiting for a long time. Finally we have literature on the Redemptive Leadership concept, a relatively new concept among leadership theorists and researchers. This model of leadership will prepare leaders to flourish in and out of a crisis. Instead of leaders facing the crisis points in their lives with shame or fear, or covering up and hiding behind their abilities and skills to deal with the crisis, they will open up and embrace the crisis. Then, those crisis moments become redemptive moments in that particular situation, and actually become the catalysts for future opportunities of leadership growth in the life of the leader. I trust that this masterpiece by Dr. Harvey Powers will powerfully fill the gap we have all been waiting for in our understanding of leadership growth and dealing with crisis moments in our lives.

—*Charles B. Mugisha, founder and president, Africa New Life Ministries, Rwanda*

Through biblical reflection upon the lived experiences of leaders, Dr. Harv Powers enables us to better understand how God is at work in us, shaping us to be the people and leaders He designed us to be. Many leaders will resonate with the Redemptive Leadership Model as Powers addresses the soul-searching questions that persist for resolutions in the midst of real-life demands on leaders.

—Jeff Denlinger, president, WorldVenture

For more than ten years now, Dr. Powers has guided me in my leadership journey using the ideas that this book captures. I've had fun seasons of great influence and painful seasons of crisis and failure. Only upon stepping back, which Harv invites me to do often, can I see how God is using crises to bring me to new stages of leadership. And as I walk my own journey, this book helps me to see crisis as an opportunity for growth in the lives of other friends and leaders whom I'm privileged to influence.

—Matt Mancinelli, CEO, Soar Detroit

REDEMPTIVE LEADERSHIP

Unleashing Your Greatest Influence

by

Dr. Harv Powers

REDEMPTIVE LEADERSHIP

Published by
Illumify Media Global
www.IllumifyMedia.com
"Write. Publish. Market. *SELL!*"

Paperback ISBN: 978-1-949021-23-3
eBook ISBN: 978-1-949021-24-0

CONTENTS

INTRODUCTION

GOD ONLY USES BROKEN LEADERS

*God is looking for broken people. When He wants
anything done, He takes up people who have come
to the end of themselves, whose confidence is not in
themselves, but in God.*

—Harry Ironside

Michael's Story

FOR WEEKS THE QUESTION pestered him, clamoring
for his attention like the service engine light on his car.
And for weeks he avoided it, evaded it, pushed it aside. But
now, as Michael began his hour-long commute home, he
turned off his cell phone and the stereo. He hadn't driven
home in silence for years. Why start today? Especially
today? That afternoon he closed the biggest deal of his
career. He should have been burning through minutes
on his cell phone like kindling—following up on details,
celebrating with friends, bragging to associates. But in the
quiet it materialized . . .

Does my life really matter?

Michael knew why he avoided the question—the answer terrified him. For all his responsibilities at work—not to mention the pressure he felt to perform—he always assumed he was doing something important. But really, what were his accomplishments? Made himself and his company a lot of money. As a matter of fact, though, he was hard-pressed to say how his product truly helped anyone beyond making life more convenient. But his coworkers looked up to him and his team needed his leadership.

Then he considered his family. Now there was an organization that needed his leadership. Most nights, though, they would have settled for his presence. Michael thought back over all the missed dinners and outings. For years he justified twelve-hour workdays by reminding himself (and occasionally his wife) food was always on the table and clothes were always in the closet. Was that really why he worked so hard? If the only concern were paying the bills, a thousand other jobs could do that.

A thousand other jobs. Did he really believe that? Could he actually do something else? Wait a minute, he didn't want to do something else. He landed a big fish today! What was the problem?

The problem was that gut-wrenching hollowness. The feeling that while his work made money, it made no difference in people's lives. *Our products will be made, sold, bought, and used . . . but by whom? People.*

Michael smiled. He wasn't noble, a martyr, or a missionary. He just wanted his work to mean something.

And he was starting to realize that meant influencing people, not just making a buck. His mind whirled with the possibilities: quitting his job—he'd saved enough to live on for years—or getting a different job, maybe working with a nonprofit, heck, maybe making more money and setting up a foundation.

Then he thought of his team. Michael had trained most of them, and he was pretty sure they all respected him. What would it be like if he led them somewhere more important than the next deal? What if he started right where he was?

Jamie's Story

Jamie sat on the dais, unable to believe she survived the last few years. Sometimes it felt like graduate school saved her life. She had charged into her public policy program with righteous anger and a zeal for advocacy. She was going to change the world. She had observed enough people who were homeless, poor, and wounded to know she wanted to lift them out of their circumstances. But she was unaware of her own need for healing.

School advanced well the first year. Jamie grew more passionate in her calling to the poor, excelled academically, and received the attention of some prominent faculty. By her second year, though, her life began to falter. Grades started slipping and she didn't want to get out of bed most days. She tumbled into clinical depression and began bingeing and purging, which she hadn't done for over ten years.

And then came the memories. First just a trickle, then a river, the memories of her past abuse soon flooded every waking moment. Thoughts of her uncle's abuse overwhelmed her. Finally, Jamie took her friend's advice to seek therapy at the university's counseling center.

"Where does your worth come from?" her counselor asked at her first session. Jamie's response was immediate. "I have no worth." She couldn't shake the feeling she was damaged goods. When she entered school, she envisioned many professional successes—developing cutting-edge programs, emerging as a leader in her field. But her first day in counseling, all that seemed impossible. All she could think was that her talents were evaporating and she would never succeed in what she thought was a lifelong calling.

After that first session with her counselor, Jamie worked hard to prove those thoughts wrong. Her grades picked up. She worked among the people who inspired her to enroll in graduate school—the homeless, the addicted, the hurting. Now she counted herself as one of them.

The hardest part was not knowing the future. She always imagined she could predict, if not control, what would happen. But now Jamie just wanted to take the next step in her calling, whatever that looked like. Sitting on the dais in her cap and gown, she heard her name called. Whatever else would happen, her next steps would be across the stage.

Joel's Story

At a conference three months prior, Pastor Joel accepted a woman's invitation to go to her room. *I now know what it feels like to cross the line*, he had thought to himself. He had compartmentalized his life for so long, his immoral behavior seemed entirely separate from his ministry and family. Burnout settled him into a comfortable numbness. Saying yes to her was the most intense feeling he had experienced in years. He continued to say yes, emailing through a new account he kept secret and arranging to meet her about once a month.

Yesterday, Pastor Joel's wife discovered his affair. *So this is what it feels like to lose everything.* Everything—his wife, his children, his ministry, his friends. It's funny how you have no idea what you're holding in your hands until it vanishes.

Yesterday felt like a dream; he could barely remember the details of what happened—Janice screaming at him, calls from the elders and denomination heads, the late-night meeting. He withdrew into a protective shell. He packed up his office while the board "considered the situation," and the possible consequences finally began to dawn on him. Everyone was reacting to news they learned about only hours ago. But Joel had been living with it for three months. In some odd way, he felt relieved to come out of hiding.

Where do I go from here? He had no idea. A year before, he had actually counseled a man in almost identical circumstances. "Pray," the righteous pastor suggested to the unfortunate parishioner. Joel smiled at the memory. How rich—his spiritual disconnection had permeated him for months. The sad part was that now, only now, he might actually have something to say—authentic and real, if not helpful—to that man.

Joel stopped packing for a moment. The weight of the thought hit him full force:

I might never again have the opportunity to talk to such a man.

The Hard Questions Demand Answers

Will God ever use me again?
How can I invest my broken life?
Does my life matter?

Have you ever asked questions like these? If you've ever held a leadership position, or desired to lead others, these questions carry a powerful charge.

Taking inventory of our lives—summing up not only our successes but also our failures—can overwhelm us and read like a damage report. Broken marriages. Failed businesses. Poor parenting, received or given. Sometimes, as in Jamie's case, we don't see many losses on our record, but we're certain we'll rack them up quickly enough. When we view our lives through such a lens, we're bound to think we will be inadequate as leaders.

This book is written for three kinds of leaders: emerging, existing, and re-emerging. The roles these types of leaders play vary, from pastor to parent to CEO; some are moving toward leadership for the first time and others are returning to it after being derailed.

As an emerging leader, Jamie needs hope. She acknowledges her abilities but wonders if God can use them. She hasn't "failed" as a leader but nevertheless feels fractured by her past and holds herself back from exerting more influence. She needs to know the sequence of development, that she fits into a process.

Michael also needs hope. Sooner or later, crisis impacts existing leaders like him, often in the middle of extraordinary success. The crisis feels like hitting "the wall" of meaning. Leaders in this position ask questions similar to Michael's. *Is this all there is? Am I making a difference?* Leaders in this season must find a way to "re-enter" leadership from a different perspective.

Then there's Pastor Joel. If he ever wants to influence people again, he too will be a re-emerging leader. A crisis on the order of a moral failure always disrupts leaders' lives, forcing them to ask a different set of questions. *Is there any hope of salvaging my life, let alone my ministry or career? Will God ever use me again?* These questions evidence the wildfire roaring through their lives.

Fire Serves a Purpose

I live in Colorado, where summer fires pose a continuous threat to people living in the dry foothills of the Rocky Mountains. During a recent fire, about eighteen thousand acres and 347 homes were ravaged over several days. One resident described being whisked off to another location as a fire bore down on her neighborhood. Far from the fire but able to watch it on television, she helplessly witnessed the flames consume her family's home. I've heard similar descriptions from many leaders caught in crises stemming from affairs, health issues, conflict, porn addiction, marital problems, burnout, or financial impropriety. The consequences of their behaviors consume everything around them, leaving them impotent to do anything but watch it burn.

That's what fire does: it burns. At first, all we see is the tragedy. But fires accomplish more than destruction. As a matter of fact, they supply a necessary component in keeping forests healthy. They burn out disease and reduce the buildup of fuels. By consuming undergrowth and invasive plant species, fires help forests become resistant to disease. Not only that, but underneath the scorched remains, new life is already growing. Some forms of pine cones can only germinate under conditions of extreme heat. And just as new life emerges from a fire's debris, hope waits to spring from a leader's failures and crises.

Redemptive Authority Can Emerge from Ashes

Redemptive Leadership rests on this hope, not just of rubble being salvaged but of transcendent influence emerging from the wreckage. Jesus said a kernel of wheat must fall to the ground and die before it produces many seeds (John 12:24). Similarly, the best leadership often springs from the ashes. None of the people in our vignettes stragically planned their crucible. At first glance, leadership influence appears forfeited. After a crisis hits, recovery seems impossible. But what we initially think about these events may prove to be only part of the story. Looking more closely, we may see the beginnings of a new kind of life. A new kind of leadership.

I decided to write this book because many leaders see this kind of turning point after a crisis as the end point. Unforeseen events intrude in their lives, crisis wreaks havoc on their organizations and families, and they stop leading. Highly competent people can no longer lead only out of their competencies alone, and they don't know how else to lead.

I believe God uses *all* the events of our lives, both positive and negative, to forge in us our redemptive influence for His kingdom. If the gospel holds any power at all, it does so because God works powerfully in and through our weakness. Paul illustrated this in 2 Corinthians 12:9: "And He has said to me, 'My grace is sufficient for you, for power is perfected in weakness.' Most gladly, therefore, I will rather boast about my weaknesses, so that the power of Christ may dwell in me."

The promise of redemption lies at the heart of the gospel. It doesn't mean God wipes the slate clean; it means he uses all the elements of our lives for His redemptive purposes. This truth conveys powerful implications for leaders. It means that God uses us not *in spite* of but *because of* our weakness. Rather than our failures being swept under the rug, they can actually aid us in our efforts to influence people. Paul wrote,

> God uses *all* the events of our lives, both positive and negative, to forge in us our redemptive influence for His kingdom.

> Even though I was formerly a blasphemer and a persecutor and a violent aggressor. Yet I was shown mercy . . . . It is a trustworthy statement, deserving full acceptance, that Christ Jesus came into the world to save sinners, among whom I am foremost of all. Yet for this reason I found mercy, so that in me as the foremost, Jesus Christ might demonstrate His perfect patience as an example for those who would believe in Him for eternal life. (1 Timothy 1:13–16)

Paul explains that his failures (sins) became, through the redemptive power of Christ, his authoritative credential to speak hope into others' lives. Does this seem counterintuitive? Redemptive processes are in fact radically counterintuitive. Current leadership culture posits that significant influence comes only through exceptional performance. In fact, most leadership literature views competency as the summit of leadership development. To be clear, I am all for competency. I propose, however, that competency falls far short of the summit of leadership development. In this book, I want to offer a model of leadership development based on redemptive bedrock.

Redemptive Leadership Catalyzes Hope

The Redemptive Leadership Model goes much deeper than how we typically think of leadership. If success consists in racking up points on the score card and playing down our failures, then very few of us are successful in a biblical sense. We may be able to hide our down side for a time, but even if others believe we have it all under control, we know differently. Redemptive leadership, on the other hand, is a framework in which God uses not only our competencies and strengths but our failures as well.

Just like the apostle Paul or King David, we too can allow God to use the dark moments in our lives, the trails covered in ashes, to help us grow. We must grow continually as leaders. We never arrive. We navigate a lifelong formation process as leaders. At each stage we gain new competencies, glean new meaning, face the crisis points in our lives, and discover (often painfully) the ways in which we still need to grow.

Counterintuitively, God uses these very events to unleash our redemptive influence. This means as God redeems the events of our lives, He works through us to catalyze redemption in the lives of those people in our care—those whom we influence or lead. This requires us to "see" differently as leaders. As we do, we can help others "see" differently as well. We can help the Michaels of the world see their crisis of meaning in a different way, help the Jamies to view their past experiences through different eyes, or help the Pastor Joels to come to see their circumstances as a beginning and not an end through God's redemptive process. Hope. Redemptive influence accesses the hope of God brought about by the death of His son.

In the coming chapters of this book, I will unpack the Redemptive Leadership Model. In chapter 1 we will explore the developmental foundations that underpin the model. Chapter 2 will give an overview of the model and examine the first two stages: competency and principle/intelligence. Competency is the entry point of leadership influence in this model. It involves the skills and experience that make leaders effective. The principle/intelligence stage transcends leadership skills and addresses the way leaders think . . . their framework, their mindset. The character stage of leadership development, discussed in chapter 3, will look at the deeper structures of a leader's life. Chapter 4 will unpack how these deeper structures shift throughout the transformation stage. The redemptive stage, covered in chapter 5, involves the miracle of redemptive influence—how God uses the broken places in our lives, through His Sprit, to speak hope into the lives of those we lead.

Before moving ahead, consider this statement: Leadership influence is formed through a developmental process. We will unpack what this means in chapter 1.

> Redemptive influence is about offering and accessing the hope of God brought about by the death of His son.

Introduction Reflection Questions

At the end of each chapter I will offer a few reflection questions. These can be used individually as a journaling prompt or as a conversation starter for you and a friend or for your team.

1. Take a moment to reflect on the title for this introduction chapter: "God Only Uses Broken Leaders." How did this idea strike you at first? How did reading the rest of the chapter expand your thoughts?

2. Which of the three opening stories (Michael, Jamie, or Joel) did you resonate with most and why?

3. Consider this quote: "God uses us not *in spite of* but *because of* our weakness." How have you seen this demonstrated in your own life or someone else's life?

4. What is one takeaway from this chapter that you want to hold on to?

CHAPTER 1

NO LEADER STARTS FULLY FORMED

Leadership is a lifetime of God's Lessons.

—*Bobby Clinton*

I LOOKED INTIMIDATING IN my Tae Kwon Do uniform, especially with the belt securely fastened around my waist. When I started flying through the air throwing spinning back kicks followed by axe kicks, it became clear who was going to win this fight. Or any fight.

Yes, this greatly impressed my six-year-old daughter.

As happens with girls her age, Hannah increasingly grew wary of strangers. She saw a news story on TV and became terrified a burglar might break into our house and hurt our family. I decided it was important to show her Dad was not going to let that happen. So, I suited up in my martial arts uniform and punched and postured my way through the house. Over the years I've told my daughter a million times that I'd keep her safe, but declaring "I love you and you are safe" with a roundhouse kick to an imaginary attacker's head bolsters credibility. And it worked. She followed me around the house, increasingly confident I could protect her.

When we reached the family room, my thirteen-year-old daughter, Courtney, responded in a slightly different manner. Briefly glancing at me then turning back to the TV, she rolled her eyes and muttered, "Hey, Jet Li, you'd better hope the bad guy doesn't have a gun!"

God Designed Developmental Growth

What was the difference between my two children? Why the wide gap in their reactions? Six-year-olds and thirteen-year-olds are miles apart *developmentally*. They both see me as their dad, but Hannah sees me as the most important and powerful man on Earth. I can do no wrong and will allow no harm. I possess, by virtue of being bigger and older, special knowledge or power to always keep her safe. In her eyes, I have "arrived" because I am an adult.

Courtney, because of her maturity, views me differently. She recognizes I wasn't born with martial arts skills nor did I magically receive them when I became an adult; I trained in them over many years. She acknowledges that I, too, am in a developmental process and have not arrived.

Leadership, likewise, must be cultivated. While "born leaders" may exist, no leader starts fully formed. At some level this may seem obvious. We realize leaders need to practice their skills and learn by making mistakes, but we seldom think of leadership as being truly developmental.

Maturational forces dictate how we grow, but we usually fail to see these dynamics operating.

Let's look more closely at development in children. Adults know children grow into adulthood. Children, however, don't see the maturing process at work. Adults seem like extraordinary beings to young children. First of all, they're big. Adults tower like giants to a small child. A grown-up's presence inspires a sense of safety in children because adults' physical power seems limitless. As a child grows to seven or eight years old, another dynamic with adults looms large: grown-ups seem to always know what to do and when to do it. They have life figured out. Though as adults we may find this absurd, children nevertheless perceive adults in this way.

> While "born leaders" may exist, no leader starts fully formed.

Despite evidence to the contrary, why do children persist in this belief? Because their developmental needs for safety and stability could not be satisfied if they believed otherwise. Without this belief, children would carry burdens they are not equipped to bear. They would battle monsters beneath their bed alone. They wouldn't know how to use a hot stove and bathe themselves safely.

In other words, children would feel the weight of adult responsibility overloading their small shoulders— and children cannot bear this burden. Not because they're stupid or weak or inferior to adults, but because *developmentally*, children differ from adults. This maturational difference makes children who they are: children. The same kind of difference distinguishes adolescents from toddlers and middle-aged adults from senior citizens. Maturation deepens and expands how we think, behave, and see the world. Growth occurs gradually and inevitably. Developmental dynamics are integral to human functioning because God has hardwired development into us.

Do children perceive growth in this manner? Not by a long shot. How does the typical child view the transition into adulthood? Kind of like a scene from *The Matrix* where Neo plugs into a computer and downloads kung fu into his brain—instant expertise. Instead of needing years of grueling training and thousands of mistakes to earn a black belt, *The* Matrix presents the notion that you just need a data dump instead of the lengthy process of maturation. Similarly, adolescents think they can read an instruction manual, pass some test, and become a mature adult. As an adult, they believe, you will always know the right action to take. Adulthood, in this view, becomes an arrival point and not a maturational journey.

Adults view adulthood differently, don't they? They view adulthood more like this: You acquire some basic skills and knowledge, and engage in learning over your life span, often by making mistakes. There are always limitations to your knowledge, but you make the best decisions you can with the information you have. Results are never guaranteed, and few formulas exist.

When we frame adulthood as a formative process, we can remain grounded when our decisions generate undesired ripples. Instead we often return to *Matrix*-like thinking and wonder what glitch in the software prevented the decision from working out. Or worse, we define ourselves as inadequate or pathological. *I should have known better. I must be blind because I missed the obvious. I'm stupid. I've been doing this awhile; I should know all there is to know.* We put ourselves in terrible binds judging ourselves harshly. Sometimes we may think God defaulted on His end of the bargain.

The Bible Uses Developmental Language

The language of growth and development is woven through the Scriptures. For example, in 2 Peter 1:5–9 (NIV), Peter writes,

> For this very reason, make every effort to add to your faith goodness; and to goodness, knowledge; and to knowledge, self-control; and to self-control, perseverance; and to perseverance, godliness; and to godliness, mutual affection; and to mutual affection, love. For if you possess these qualities in increasing measure, they will keep you from being ineffective and unproductive in your

knowledge of our Lord Jesus Christ. But whoever does not have them is nearsighted and blind, and forgetting that they been cleansed from their past sins.

Note the progression? Peter exhorts his readers to actively engage in a growth process—*make every effort* with the focus of progressively *adding* each of the qualities listed to the previous.

Peter creates a powerful sequence. By adding each quality—knowledge, perseverance, and love—to faith, the quality of our faith shifts. Mixing alloys one by one into metal makes a stronger substance. Without the alloys, the metal remains weaker; without *these qualities*, our faith remains shortsighted or less mature. In other words, faith does not come fully developed.

Paul uses developmental language when writing to the Ephesian church about the maturation process (see Ephesians 4:12). He says we must become "mature, attaining to the whole measure of the fullness of Christ" (Ephesians 4:13 NIV). This makes sense, doesn't it? That's what bodies do—they mature. In maturity they attain their fullness; this occurs when their ability to run and lift and balance reaches its greatest capability. Without maturity, we can experience the presence of Christ. With maturity, we expand our capacity to experience the *fullness* of Christ. When we proceed through the developmental process, "we will no longer be infants, tossed back and forth" by the deceit and scheming of others (Ephesians 4:14 NIV). Maturity fosters increasing stability and wise judgment.

Leadership Influence Matures through Stages

The struggle to embrace the developmental process is common to most of us in the arenas of leadership, parenting, marriage, and career, among others. In my work as a clinical supervisor for psychotherapists, I often observe this dynamic. Almost without exception, students believe graduate school should sufficiently equip them to be competent therapists. Soon enough, they discover it does not. Graduate school provides the basic knowledge of assessment, diagnostics, and treatment, but it can't hand-deliver the skills and instinct of a mature therapist. What develops them? Clinical experience, mentoring, and supervision. It's the only route. We must *grow* into competent therapists.

Like everyone I supervise, I needed to learn this the hard way too. The first time a client sat across from me, I felt like I had no idea what to do. In reality I did have wisdom to offer. Even in the very first session, I wasn't completely clueless, but I wasn't fully competent either. God uses us where we are, and we can

> God has woven the developmental process into the fabric of creative design so we can grow more fully into the people He has crafted us to be.

be grateful He does. God has woven the developmental process into the fabric of creative design so we can grow more fully into the people He has crafted us to be.

Models of Developmental Process

Before we talk about the model of redemptive leadership in the next chapter, it will help us to first get a handle on a model of development. This model is not new but a summarized version of development in the broadest sense. Researchers such as Erik Erikson, Jean Piaget, and Lawrence Kohlberg, to name a few, devised models that map different aspects of human development— intellectual, social, and moral. Understanding these models will forge a foundation for our discussion in later chapters.

At its most basic level, development looks like stair steps:

This visual illustrates the progressive nature of development: each step builds and depends upon the previous step. Many developmental models use the notion of stages rather than steps. Each stage cultivates the skills and maturity foundational to the next stage. Each subsequent stage incorporates the learning from a previous stage in order to accomplish the developmental tasks of the new stage. Learning attained in a previous stage blends with the subsequent stage to generate a qualitative shift, transcending what came before.

A leader's development of listening skills provides a great example. Clark, a senior leader in a midsized organization, sounded bewildered when he sought me out for coaching. Feedback from coworker evaluations indicated his senior staff did not feel heard. Team motivation had declined stemming from a hairline trust fracture in the team's culture. Clark was a typical senior leader. He preferred getting to the bottom line of an issue in the most direct route possible. He had learned to *listen* for relevant facts and dispense decisions, solutions, and advice with economical precision.

"Of course I listen!" he protested to me. "I am an expert at listening! I can get to the crux of an issue as effectively as anyone I know. It's what's made me so successful in leading my organization!"

In some ways, Clark was right. He excelled at getting to the bottom line—*problem-solving listening*— but floundered at *relational listening*. He struggled to hear *below the content* to the *relational impact* of his delivery. His senior leaders conceded he got the facts straight, but they were trying to say they felt marginalized as people.

As you might guess, we explored how this manifested itself outside of work and learned that his wife and kids often felt similarly. Had Clark learned to listen? Yes, at one level. His team, however, was asking him to listen at a new *developmental* level. Did Clark need to jettison his problem-solving skills? No, of course not! He did need to advance to a new, deeper stage of listening. Both his team and his spouse welcomed his new growth.

Each Stage Is Essential

Looking through this lens, it's tempting to think of some stages as better than others, especially when we haven't progressed to the point we'd like to. But who of my supervisees, just out of graduate school, could exhibit the developmental level of a therapist who's been practicing for thirty-five years? Are recent graduates inferior? No, of course not! Every mature therapist begins the same way, as a recent graduate gaining experience over time. To view my stage of development as better would be like saying it's better to think abstractly like a twenty-year-old than concretely like a two-year-old, or that it's better to be retired than operate in one's thirties. When thinking developmentally, remember, each stage serves an essential function.

Here, our stair step visual may be problematic. If a leader needs to "revisit a stair," how can we show that without implying regression? If she's gaining new skills and new growth, then clearly she is not losing ground developmentally.

The image of stair steps reflects the classic development model, but still, it's incomplete. As we try to describe more adequately what development looks like, remember that all models *attempt* to describe reality but cannot comprehensively define it. As soon as we think otherwise, we start trying to cram the events of real life into our framework, rather than letting our understanding flow from what we actually observe.

A stairway implies a linear structure made up of progression, sequence, and a sense of forward movement. How do we represent nonlinear growth, i.e., when growth in one area ripples into another? That's a common occurrence. For example, when we work out, developing our body, the effects make us feel better about ourselves emotionally. To construct a comprehensive model for the stages of development requires more of a tapestry than a linear drawing. Clearly, one image is not enough. It's easy to see why Jesus used so many different images and metaphors in describing what growth looks like: a seed planted and growing; a seed falling to the ground and dying; a rebellious teenager leaving home and then returning, a new man; a woman experiencing a redemptive encounter at a well that changed her forever.

Development Progresses in Spirals

So now we understand better why stair steps are inadequate to describe reality. If we could somehow combine stair steps, stages, a tapestry, and Jesus' word pictures, we just might possess a preferred framework. In lieu of such a complex paradigm, let's add to our stair steps an element of circularity, or return, like a spiral:

In our growth as people or as leaders, we not only incorporate what we've learned previously into what we're learning now, but we also go back and revisit what we've learned or experienced. This doesn't mean we've lost ground. It means we're growing and developing.

Spiritual maturity occurs in the same manner. For many of us, following Christ means learning to trust God in entirely new ways. We trust that God exists, that He desires good for us, and that we're forgiven. Now, let me ask those of you who have been Christians for more than ten years: Do you trust God the same way you learned to trust Him when you started following Christ? You're likely trusting Him in both similar and in much more profound ways.

What does it mean, at thirty-something, to trust that God desires good for me after I've already experienced a ministry blowup, a betrayal by a friend, a significant personal failure, or a layoff, all life events not even on the horizon when I was twenty-five? Whatever it involves, I am not starting over—I'm not trusting God for the first time, as if the last ten years never happened. I bring with me the trust I first learned at the beginning of my spiritual walk, even though I exercise a different kind of trust now. I accept God's kindness toward me, even though I have experienced pain. If I didn't believe in God's faithfulness, I would exhibit the most infantile, undeveloped kind of faith. To recognize God working good in my life after I've been laid off reveals an expanded and deepened understanding of trusting in God. It means trusting God to use the difficult events of my life redemptively.

You Can't Fast-Track Development

By now it should be clear that fast-tracking doesn't work when it comes to leadership development. We cannot rush developmental progression any more than we can rush a crop of corn. It's not for lack of trying. Some leadership models, especially those primarily competency-based, emphasize the importance of training and acquiring new skills as fast as possible. As I already mentioned, I'm in favor of skill acquisition. But our culture reinforces the belief that we can speed up growth, compress it, or fast-track it if only we work hard enough, are bright enough, or show up early enough. This often manifests *Matrix* thinking, the belief we can somehow circumvent the maturational process.

Whether in leadership or in marriage, you can't master its art by attending a couple weekend seminars or by reading a book on the six principles of success. Developmental processes do not work that way. Instead God, in His infinite wisdom, uses the events of our lives, both positive and negative, to shape our leadership influence in ways we could never foresee.

> We cannot rush developmental progression any more than we can rush a crop of corn.

This process becomes apparent in the lives of Michael, Jamie, Pastor Joel, and Joseph of the Old Testament.

We meet Joseph in depth at about age seventeen. Most of us, at seventeen, are ill-prepared for the realities of living an adult life. Chapters 37 through 50 of Genesis walk us through a story of intrigue, profound disappointment, and redemptive revelation. In an instant, Joseph's previous life shatters. Ten older brothers hold him captive in a well as they decide his fate. This sets in motion a series of events of tragic proportions and unforeseen impact. Genesis chronicles Joseph being sold into slavery, getting transported into another culture, becoming a manager in a wealthy home, rising in stature to administer a prison, and finally assuming the role of comptroller of Egypt.

Joseph learns again and again to trust God throughout his journey. He learns that God has not forgotten him in a well, in Potiphar's house, in a prison cell, or as a steward for one of the most powerful nations of its time. Each new season taught Joseph about himself, God, and the deeper journey of faith. Each event became formative, shaping him for his greatest redemptive impact.

We know how the story ends. Joseph's brothers believe they deserve retribution, and their politically powerful brother has the means to carry it out. He doesn't. In a moment of profound insight he says, "You intended to harm me, but God intended it for good to accomplish what is now being done, the saving of many lives" (Genesis 50:20 NIV). *God intended it for good.* God *redeemed* Joseph's situation—He used Joseph's captivity to set others free. He unleashed Joseph's leadership influence for a greater good. Could any of this have happened if

Joseph had not been sold into slavery? No. God used Joseph *because* of his circumstances, not *in spite* of them. He teaches Joseph to *see with different eyes*—to see redemptively.

Note that Joseph possessed skills. Note too that God used the circumstances of Joseph's life, even the tragic ones, to develop those skills into competencies. Organizing, supervising others, strategic planning, managing people, forecasting, and interpreting dreams, to name a few. The development of these skills into competencies allowed him to become successful in all he did. Joseph didn't come fully formed at seventeen. Counterintuitively, the tragic events of his early life set in motion the very growth plan that led to his greatest impact. Joseph illustrates the very developmental process we have been discussing.

> God used Joseph *because* of his circumstances, not *in spite* of them.

My Own Development Revealed

Years ago I had an experience that illustrates what Peter (2 Peter 1:5–9) and Paul (Ephesians 4:13) describe about the maturational process. It also points out my developmental deficits at the time. I was interning at a church in inner-city Philadelphia. On one occasion, I led a team that shared the gospel door-to-door with the people in our community. My partner and I entered a crumbling apartment building and started knocking on doors. No one answered on our first several attempts, but finally a man called out, "Just a minute!" in a deep voice. We stood for a full minute before a large, muscled, tattooed man opened the door. I introduced myself as a pastor from the church down the street, and he invited us in.

We sat down and his story began to unfold. His name was John and he lived in the apartment with his girlfriend. He had just been released from prison two weeks before and was trying to get on his feet. Right about then I started thinking, *Wow! You never know what kind of journey lies behind each door you knock on.*

As events progressed, Jim and I shared the gospel with John. And wouldn't you know it, he embraced it. Who knows what prepared his heart for that moment? I can only imagine the emotions associated with just being released from prison and beginning to taste a fresh start and the potential for a new life. I can also imagine the fear and uncertainty with this kind of new beginning.

"Guys, would you mind talking to my girlfriend?" John asked. "I think she'll have questions about the Bible I can't answer."

"Sure, John!" Jim responded. "Can we set up a time to come back and meet her?"

"Hey, Natalie!" John called out. "I want you to meet these guys." We had no idea she was in the next room. After a short conversation, Natalie received Christ too. What a wonderful, sacred moment. That's when my lack of understanding developmental processes collided with this God moment. John and Natalie, now believers for less than five minutes, were unmarried and living together.

In retrospect, I so regret what happened next. In a well-intentioned and gentle manner, we explained that if they wanted to take their new life in Christ seriously, they could not live together. John and Natalie very much wanted to take their newfound faith seriously, and they agreed to separate. Before the afternoon was over, we had called the church and made arrangements for Natalie to stay in a small apartment in the parsonage.

Looking back on that day, as grateful as I am for that couple's spiritual receptivity, I wish I had been sensitive to the fact they were infant believers. Before the end of the week, Jim and I understood how critical this was. Unfortunately, we realized it too late. Natalie soon moved out of the parsonage, and despite repeated attempts, we were never able to reach her or John again.

Please don't misunderstand: sexual purity is important, and there's nothing wrong with door-to-door evangelism. But as complete strangers, Jim and I walked all over their boundaries and asked them—told them, really—to do too much, too fast. We instructed them to take action for which they were not developmentally ready, in the midst of a major life transition—John getting out of prison. Their difficulty in maintaining our prescribed living arrangement did not reflect a lack of sincerity; they demonstrated their willingness to repent from the moment we met them. Instead, the "problem" they experienced in living apart was akin to the "problem" a toddler encounters with riding a two-wheeler—it's too soon. We short-circuited their developmental process. Returning to our metaphor of a forest fire and its aftermath, what I asked of John and Natalie was like asking a seedling in the ashes to get busy and produce fruit now.

The Day I learned a Crucial Lesson

Let's set aside this couple's development and look at my own. In some ways I was mature that day in John's apartment, but not as mature as I am now. More mature than John and Natalie, for example, evidenced by my knowledge that premarital sex falls outside God's plan for relationships. So today, in my current stage of development, I would recognize John and Natalie's need for support and nurturing in their new faith and their life transitions. I would focus more on the first principles of faith, like joining a community of believers and trusting that community to care for them. I would encourage them to get to know God through His Word and remind myself to be patient, watching for the Spirit of God to catalyze their growth.

I wasn't a bad leader that day, just like John wasn't a bad newborn Christian because he was unmarried. I wanted to honor Christ and do what was best for that couple, and I tried to guide them with the resources I had at the time. One of my resources was competency. I knew how to effectively share the gospel and quickly solve their cohabitation problem. But since then, I have developed other resources. In addition to my competencies, I can now discern, informed by developmental readiness, whether an action *should* be taken at a particular moment. Today I would see John and Natalie's cohabitation not as a problem to be solved but as a growth issue I might be privileged to guide them through over time.

Mature leadership requires far more than competency. Forged by entering the crucible of their own development, leaders must gain a deeper wisdom, which is seldom addressed in leadership seminars. I call this process the Redemptive Leadership Model. Those who work through its stages will be leaders equipped to release their redemptive influence for God's purposes. I will now unpack its stages in the coming chapters.

Chapter 1 Reflection Questions

1. Consider the quote "While born leaders may exist, no leader starts fully formed." What does this look like in your life, and what does it mean to you as a leader?

2. Where would you place yourself in your own developmental process?

3. Consider the quote "We cannot rush developmental progression any more than we

can rush a crop of corn." Agree or disagree? Why or why not? If true, what are the implications for you and those under your care?

4. What is your takeaway from this chapter?

CHAPTER 2

COMPETENCY AND PRINCIPLE/ INTELLIGENCE: INFLUENCE THAT MATTERS

A life is not important except in the impact it has on other lives.

—*Jackie Robinson*

Do you remember how you began as a leader? Maybe you excelled in your field and coworkers began seeking the "secrets" of your success. You became the go-to person for coaching and leadership advice. Or a respected colleague recognized your potential and created opportunities cultivating your skills. Or perhaps an influential person became the role model you wanted to emulate. Without knowing it, they seeded a hunger in you to learn about leadership and this started your journey.

More than thirty years ago, I began studying leadership as the focus of my doctoral dissertation. Since that start, in my role as a psychologist and consultant I have continued mining the stories of leaders. Emerging leaders, experienced leaders, and re-emerging leaders imparted to me a pragmatic education in lessons hard-won across the stages of leadership. These real men and women inspired the following questions: How do most leaders start their journey? What common ingredients serve as developing influences in a leader's life? What key factors differentiate effective leaders? What predictable patterns emerge in the process of leadership development? This chapter will articulate the initial stages of leadership influence.

Who Has Positively Influenced Your Life?

I've posed this question to hundreds of leaders over three decades: Who has been the most influential leader in your life and what made them so? These individuals included leaders from their late teens to their early eighties, from both genders, from beginning to expert, and from various spheres of leadership: business, military, government, churches, and para-church ministries. I've polled re-emerging leaders as well, and similar themes consistently emerge:

Key influencers, beset with demanding schedules, made relationship building a high priority. As a result, the leaders' accessibility and willingness to spend time with their subordinates in non-work activities helped them feel known.

Key influencers authentically cared for their subordinates. In response to this question, individuals repeatedly told stories illustrating the care that mentors exhibited toward them—often never stated directly but powerfully communicated in actions. "He would call me to check in on me." "She asked about my family." "He would eat lunch with me at this outdoor table near our office and we talked about life." Genuine care, intangible though it might seem, powerfully influences followers.

Key influencers realized the potential in colleagues and inspired them to believe in themselves. Can you relate to the potency of a respected leader believing in you? When they see your potential in the midst of your self-doubt, their belief powerfully infuses

> Key influencers, beset with demanding schedules, made relationship building a high priority.

you, exhilarating and terrifying at the same time. It calls you to a higher place of stewarding your abilities. "Mary, the VP that oversaw partner relations, possessed this uncanny ability to put people in the right place. She asked me to take over a troubled team that was filled with distrust and conflict. I told her it was beyond my ability! Her belief in me allowed me to rise to the challenge and develop a whole new set of skills."

Key influencers transmitted information by "absorption" rather than "impartation." Mentees regularly told stories of life encounters where they observed their mentor in action. This allowed experiential learning, which guided the person decades later. "I remember the way John dealt with conflict. He was a master! I observed him calm people with his demeanor and the way he listened to them. I still think about him today when I deal with an employee conflict."

Key influencers stayed engaged when their mentees encountered times of crisis. Crisis points are often revelatory. They expose our doubts, failings, blind spots, and growth edges. Key influencers intuitively understand that crisis points have the potential to be key transformational windows. "My last ministry placement ended in disaster. I made a series of bad hires resulting in a severe power struggle and resigned rather than split the church. Two days later, Vernon called and invited me to breakfast. I couldn't believe it! The next year we met weekly and he breathed life into me during one of my darkest seasons. I credit his persistence as an essential factor in my being in the pastorate today."

Does a pivotal person of impact come to mind? I bet you find most of these characteristics present in that person's relationship with you. Remarkably, books on highly effective leaders rarely highlight these qualities. They almost never appear in job descriptions of senior leaders and seldom appear as essential goals of academic curriculum in leadership. These elements matter, however, and surface as integral components for those on the receiving end of good leadership.

The Story of Bob Seamore

Bob, a man in his mid to late twenties, entered my life at a crucial juncture and became a key influence. A PhD chemical engineer, Bob researched advanced plastics for the U.S. Army at Edgewood Arsenal, a base near my church. Looking back, he likely didn't realize the pivotal role he played in the cultivation of my faith during my freshman through junior years of high school, when he volunteered as our youth group leader.

Bob impacted my life, first, because of the time he spent with me. We hung out drinking Coke and eating pizza, played countless hours of tennis, listened to music, and talked. We talked a lot—about life, the world around us, the Vietnam War, dating, my family, and the Bible. Bob had this way of asking questions rather than giving answers. He asked questions which opened my mind to new ways of thinking.

Bob impacted my life through the time he spent with me, or better said, the time he made for me. He accompanied me through many crises . . . dating breakups, family conflicts, and major life decisions. Eventually, we brainstormed ministry opportunities to reach my high school friends. He often placed me in important leadership roles. We started a weekend "coffee house" (remember, this was the late '60s and early '70s) long before Starbucks. We put on concerts, published a newspaper, and led discussion groups about current music.

He believed in me and then helped me believe, too. Through him, God planted the seeds of loving God's Word and catalyzed a hunger to apply the Bible to real life. He guided me as I decided to pursue a Bible degree in college—and did this all without advising me directly. Bob indelibly marked my life, not because of his leadership technique but because of his personal investment . . . his heart was for me.

> Bob indelibly marked my life, not because of his leadership technique but because of his personal investment . . . his heart was for me.

What shaped Bob's ability to impact me so significantly? Although I don't know the specifics for him, I'm sure his influence arose from his own developmental journey.

THE FIVE STAGES OF THE REDEMPTIVE LEADERSHIP MODEL

I'll now unfold the five stages of the Redemptive Leadership Model: competency, principle/intelligence, character, transformation, and redemption. This model synthesizes the patterns gleaned from the last thirty years of my work with leaders and teaching leadership at the doctoral level. The first two stages, competency and principle/intelligence, will be explained in this chapter. The last three stages require chapters of their own, as those stages most prominently break from more mainstream models of leadership development.

The Competency Stage

Competency launches the leadership journey for most of us. We develop specific areas of expertise others recognize and value. Continued training, practice, and coaching hones our abilities and we become more effectual. Through demonstrated impact, people view us as increasingly "qualified" and "knowledgeable." At this point, they ask us to train them in our areas of proficiency. At times, these aptitudes start as natural gifts or abilities, such as public speaking.

My teacher/therapist capabilities first emerged in high school. In fact, I unknowingly became a teacher/counselor through conversations with my desk mate in ninth grade homeroom. I often read the Bible before class to feed my new faith, and Jennifer asked questions about my reading. Over the course of the year, we talked about her struggles with parents and boyfriends, and I found myself relating her life to different passages of Scripture. She often commented, "I never realized the Bible could be so practical." Nearly forty-five years have passed since that embryonic exposure.

Progressively, other students began asking me for advice. When difficulties arose, they would catch me in the hall and ask, "Can I bounce this off you?" Retrospectively, others began to recognize and validate my strengths, though I could not have articulated them at the time. I see it now as my fledgling stage of developing competency. In fact, my senior yearbook includes penned comments like these: "I'll always remember how good a listener you were." "To the guy who was always able to find the right words at the right time." "You were always there for me." These remarks bear witness to my early aptitude for hearing people at a deeper level and relating their lives meaningfully to God's Word.

Competency requires more, however, than just natural skill or ability. When effective skills become honed and seasoned by practice, they ripen into competency. Neither skill alone nor experience alone suffices.

If I recommend a surgeon to you, I am endorsing her as competent. What do I mean by that? Does she possess knowledge and skill? Certainly. She must know anatomy and physiology like the back of her hand. She must be blessed with excellent fine motor control and learn the proper technique to hold a scalpel. The fact that she graduated from medical school, however, doesn't mean she has achieved competency. Even an intellectually gifted physician needs years of practice, operating on real people, to become a master surgeon. Likewise, if a surgeon with many years in her field becomes lethargic about continuing education, her competency will decay. Neither experience alone nor knowledge nor skill alone sustains competency.

Competency Increases Our Influence

As our competencies strengthen, people begin to follow us, increasing our influence. Thus, competency defines the first stage of leadership influence and *not* its final stage. Competencies can be cultivated in an array of content areas: tax preparation, computer applications, strategic planning, operational implementation, surgery, teaching, financial investing—and we then influence others through those competencies. We can all bring to mind a person of influence who captivated us through a specific area of competency.

Attending Philadelphia College of Bible catalyzed a major turning point of my life, bringing me into contact with highly competent people. The school, located in downtown Philadelphia, contrasted enormously with the rural culture of West Virginia where I grew up.

Dr. Douglas McCorkle, the president of the school, captivated me with his competency. His messages in chapel exposed me to someone exceptionally skilled in exploring the Word of God. His quick wit, intensity, and piercing eyes mesmerized me. Instead of struggling to keep my mind on what a speaker said, for the first time I felt disappointed when Dr. McCorkle began his concluding remarks. I wanted more—more biblical characters coming alive, more insight into issues I struggled with, more understanding of the stories of victory, failure, and the way God redemptively reveals Himself to His people. I frequently felt transported to the same holy ground Moses stood on.

Over time, I became curious: *What contributed to Dr. McCorkle's effectiveness? What study skills gave him such deep insight into the Bible? How did he use spoken language to make this ancient document a living Word?* Consequently, I approached my professors with a new passion for learning. I studied inductive Bible study skills. I gained an understanding of Greek verbs and why they matter. I read about homiletics—the art and science of creating a sermon. At Philadelphia College of Bible, I gained my first exposure to how people learn and how to construct a lesson plan, which draws a student into a discovery process. I studied the flow and rhythm of teaching, in hopes of stimulating a desire to apply the learning to real life.

> Thus, competency defines the first stage of leadership influence and *not* its final stage.

I came to view learning as an interactive process—an artful dance between speaker and listener who cocreate, with the help of the Holy Spirit, a transformational window. In time, I realized that effective teaching/ preaching consisted of *learned* skills and competencies. These beliefs originated with Dr. McCorkle.

Competent Leaders Inspire Confidence

What is it like to follow competent leaders? As you observe their thinking and witness their effectiveness, your belief in their leadership expands. The leader's opinions and guidance carry increasing weight. Believing that a leader knows what he's doing forms the bedrock of their influence. Our confidence in that leader motivates us, grounds us, focuses us, and enables us to buy into a shared vision and endure hardship to make that vision a reality.

Conversely, when confidence in the leader's competency falters, the leader's ability to influence followers dwindles. President Jimmy Carter coined the phrase "Crisis of Confidence" in his famous July 15, 1979 speech. He said, "The erosion of our confidence is threatening to destroy the social and the political fabric of America." Many believe this speech actually eroded confidence in President Carter's leadership, which led to his defeat by Ronald Reagan less than a year later.

Leadership literature, both sacred and secular, tends to major on competency. Books, trainings, and seminars abound concentrating on a myriad of skills a leader must possess. These range from time management, communication, and vision casting to strategic planning, operational implementation, and managing teams by objective. Clearly, competencies serve a critical function. Eventually, however, most adept leaders reach a point where they sense a need for more. Another competency-based training holds little draw. This craving marks the transition to the second stage of development: the principle/intelligence stage of leadership.

The Principle/Intelligence Stage: Understanding the Whys Behind Our Skills

Entry into this stage marks a qualitative shift in a leader's development. While the previous stage focuses on the how-tos (in specific content areas), this stage targets the underlying reasons or principles—the whys—behind a set of skills. A leader's understanding deepens in this stage and lays the foundation for a broader scope of influence extending beyond their skills or practices.

Stephen Covey's book *The 7 Habits of Highly Effective People* popularized the notion of principles. He applied these concepts to leadership development in his 1991 book, *Principle-Centered Leadership*. He defines "principles" as "guidelines for human conduct that are proven to have enduring permanent value."[1] Principles become compass headings; they point us in the right direction. Principles possess constancy; they apply in all places at all times. Identifying and owning principles creates wisdom in leaders, which expands influence beyond formal training. Covey's well-known statement, "Seek to understand before being understood," pointedly articulates a principle. Its wisdom applies to most situations, if not all, and boosts impact. Effective listening would be a skill set; seeking to understand before being understood articulates a wisdom principle. It addresses the purpose of effective listening.

Tara, a good friend of mine, possesses polished competencies in the English language. She secured a master's degree in English, taught at the college level, and worked as a writer and editor for years. Several years ago, she began to feel a strong pull to work as a leader, developing congregational community as a member of her church's staff. Although she had never worked in this kind of a position, she understood the underlying principles. No one had ever formally taught her how to run meetings, but she grasped the need for her team to build relationships with one another while receiving guidance.

Her team felt empowered. She applied the collaborative structure she had cultivated as a writer/editor to developing new programs and communication plans in her ministry area. Tara's principle-based approach expanded her influence beyond her formal training and sphere of competency.

Intelligence Measures Our Capacity to Learn and Reason

The concept of intelligence deepens and expands our model of principle-based leadership. What do I mean by intelligence? The term IQ, familiar to most of us, stands for intelligence quotient. While made up of specific skills including math, reading, memory, and spatial problem solving, the concept transcends these specific abilities. IQ attempts to gauge a person's capacity to learn and reason.

At this point, it will be helpful to introduce the notion of *gestalt*, as the English language does not contain an equivalent word. Gestalt, a German word, represents a concept that is more than the sum of its parts and therefore creates a wholly different substance or idea.

Let me give an example. Let's say you eat chocolate, a cup of flour, a cup of sugar, a teaspoon of baking soda, two cups of milk, and some eggs. Consuming these elements individually provides one kind of culinary impact. If, however, you combine these elements in the right proportions and in the right order, then apply oven heat, the result becomes qualitatively different: chocolate cake. Thus, the end product transcends the individual elements. Gestalt captures this idea so essential to understanding leadership intelligence. Specific skills or competencies combine in such a way to generate a shift of framework, producing a new way of thinking about leadership influence. The principle/intelligence stage of leadership generates a shift beyond specific competencies to new frameworks of thinking about leadership influence.

Leadership Intelligence Contains Subtypes

Dr. Daniel Goleman's book *Emotional Intelligence* broadened our concept of intelligence. Instead of IQ alone, Goleman convincingly argued that emotional intelligence, or EI, predicted success in a particular field more than technical competency alone.[2] EI incorporates self-awareness, the ability to read others, listening under the words, and the capacity to read the emotional atmosphere of a group. Many subtypes of leadership intelligence exist—emotional intelligence, strategic intelligence, tactical intelligence, operational intelligence, cultural intelligence, conflict intelligence, and spiritual intelligence to name a few.

> The principle/ intelligence stage of leadership generates a shift beyond specific competencies to new frameworks of thinking about leadership influence.

In the principle/intelligence stage of leadership, our capacity to influence transcends our specific skill competencies. Tom earned his MBA from a major university and enjoyed many years of business success. He helped found Blockbuster Video, Boston Market, and Einstein Bagels. Tom knew firsthand the effort required to start a business: the countless hours developing systems, taking risks, hiring people and training them. Over the years, he had weathered the best of times and the worst of times in business cycles.

Through a series of circumstances, Tom and I met, formed a close friendship, and became founding partners in a ministry, The Pharos Group. Pharos focused on increasing the effectiveness of faith-based leaders and their organizations. Tom brought many proven strengths as a skilled businessperson. Often I witnessed him developing systems, which guided leaders in achieving key objectives.

He also keenly read people, which informed his capacity to establish relationships of trust.

When we, as The Pharos Group, consulted with medium to large faith-based organizations, Tom's grasp of underlying principles of assessment, coaching, and organizational systems manifested repeatedly. On one occasion, he coached a regional church leader in facilitating efficient meetings, which increased the leader's impact and mobilized his key leaders.

So while Tom had never been to seminary or operated a faith-based ministry, he identified the underlying principles that made him successful in business and applied them to ministry organizations. This was not a wholesale importing of business templates into ministry situations. Doing so would not have worked. Instead, he used his leadership intelligence to apply the wisdom gained from his background into new circumstances, which expanded Tom's bandwidth of influence. Many successful business leaders cannot make this transition. They try to utilize their business formulas without understanding a ministry culture, often alienating others, damaging trust, and impeding their effectiveness. Tom's leadership intelligence allowed him to navigate ministry culture effectively.

Intelligence-Based Leaders Deepen Understanding

At the end of *The Matrix*, a moment occurs when Neo *sees* the matrix. Prior to this scene, he has observed

the code on a monitor and observed its effects. In that
moment of revelation, his framework shifts. He under-
stands the matrix and begins
to help others to do so as
well. Forgive the analogy,
but intelligence-centered
leaders do the same for
followers: they convey un-
derstanding—understanding of why the erosion of relational trust weakens influence, why culture and context
must be grasped before change can be initiated, why the
emotional unhealth of the leader limits team performance.
Intelligence stage leaders possess a distinctive framework:
they see below the surface. They interpret events and
circumstances through the lens of the underlying
principles. They help those who follow to do the same.

> Intelligence stage leaders possess a distinctive framework: they see below the surface.

An Example Of Intelligence-Based Leadership: Dr. Martin Luther King Jr.

The Reverend Martin Luther King Jr. exemplifies
intelligence-based leadership (and so much more). Dr.
King's formal training prepared him for the pastorate.
He graduated from Crozer Theological Seminary with a
bachelor of divinity degree and Boston University where
he received his PhD in systematic theology in 1955.[3]
He began serving as the senior pastor of Dexter Avenue
Baptist Church in Montgomery, Alabama, in 1954 at the
age of twenty-five.[4]

Dr. King set out to be a pastor, not a civil rights leader or the poignant national voice of social justice. He stated in his famous *Letter from a Birmingham Jail*, "Before I was a civil rights leader, I was a preacher of the Gospel. This was my first calling and it still remains my greatest commitment. You know, actually all that I do in civil rights I do because I consider it a part of my ministry. I have no other ambitions in life but to achieve excellence in the Christian ministry."[5]

So how did a pastor with no formal training or background in organizing a movement, applying public policy, practicing law, or managing change become the preeminent leader of the civil rights movement? I believe reaching the principle/intelligence stage of leadership influence best explains his impact.

Dr. King saw the world differently than most. He knew deeply the nature of human beings and their need for a greater, nobler place. He touched the deep need of the human heart for freedom and equality. He spoke with a perception few people possessed at the time. His most famous speech, "I Have a Dream," given in front of the Lincoln Memorial in 1963, captures his vision:

> I say to you today, my friends, so even though we face the difficulties of today and tomorrow, I still have a dream. It is a dream deeply rooted in the American dream. I have a dream that

one day this nation will rise up and live out the true meaning of its creed: "We hold these truths to be self-evident: that all men are created equal." . . . I have a dream that my four little children will one day live in a nation where they will not be judged by the color of their skin but by the content of their character. I have a dream that one day . . . right there in Alabama, little black boys and black girls will be able to join hands with little white boys and white girls as sisters and brothers. I have a dream today.[6]

These lines still stir us. Some consider this speech to be one of the greatest in American oratory. It pushed the civil rights movement to the forefront of the nation's conscious Dr. King's influence broadened far beyond his training and practice as a local church pastor. In recognition of his influence, he received at least fifty honorary degrees, the Nobel Peace Prize (1964), and posthumously the Presidential Medal of Freedom (1977) from President Jimmy Carter, who stated, "Martin Luther King Jr. was the conscience of his generation. He gazed upon the great wall of segregation and saw that the power of love could bring it down....He made our nation stronger because he made it better. His dream sustains us yet."[7]

Dr. Martin Luther King Jr. demonstrated principle/intelligence-based leadership. His grasp of the principles motivating the human heart and his ability to see beyond the present widened his influence, exceeding his formal training. Granted, not all principle/intelligence-based leaders become like Martin Luther King Jr. Whatever the scope of leadership, however, this stage enlarges a leader's effect.

Our discussion of competency and principle/ intelligence-based leadership builds on the work of many others. Books abound regarding the core competencies of leaders, and many authors like Steven Covey and Daniel Goleman write about leadership principles and intelligence. I believe a leader entering the principle/intelligence stage experiences a shift in mindset that expands influence beyond competency alone. In the next few chapters we will turn our attention to the character, transformation, and redemptive stages of leadership. These stages form the distinctive crux of the Redemptive Leadership Model.

Chapter 2 Reflection Questions

1. Reflect on your own leadership journey. When did you first become aware of your influence in others' lives? How did you feel at the time?

2. Who have been the most influential leaders in your life, and what did they do to influence you? What surprises you about your answer?

3. How would you describe some of your leadership competencies? How would others describe them? Consider inviting others you trust to give you feedback about your competencies.

4. How do you relate to the concept of leadership intelligence? What examples come to mind of leaders demonstrating leadership intelligence (like emotional intelligence)?

5. What is your takeaway from this chapter?

CHAPTER 3

THE CHARACTER-BASED LEADER: A DEEPER FOUNDATION

Nearly all men can withstand adversity, but if you want to test a man's character, give him power. I desire so to conduct the affairs of this administration that if at the end, when I come to lay down the reins of power, I have lost every other friend on earth, I shall at least have one friend left, and that friend shall be down inside me.

—*Abraham Lincoln, 16th U.S. president (1809–1865)*

HE PLUNGED HEADLONG INTO the night. Terror forced him away . . . away from his position of status and power. The same terror, fused with shame, drove him forward . . . toward a foreign darkness, strange and directionless. Exhausted, spent, depleted, he collapsed on the hard ground. An inky darkness enshrouded him, thwarting his vision. *How will I ever find my way again?* Unprompted, the memories came. Snapshot vignettes of the last few days and the tipping point of decision, which changed everything . . . forever.

The well of Midian (Exodus 2:15) symbolized a profound inflection point in the trajectory of Moses' life. One morning, he awoke as a prince of Egypt, and by evening he found himself a fugitive running for his life, a nightmare from which he could not awaken. In numbed disbelief, the questions, no doubt, flooded his mind: *What happened? How did I get here? What was I thinking? If only I could take back what I did! How could I have been so shortsighted? Have I lost my usefulness to God?* The last question may seem odd, given what *we* know about the latter portion of Moses' life. Remember, Moses' future could not be seen from the well. So too we, as leaders, lose future sight when we face our own well of Midian.

Remember Pastor Joel, Michael, and Jamie from the introduction? Each, in the context of his or her life story, encountered a unique crisis point like Moses. This chapter considers the distinct well of Midian every leader must face as an *essential* component in maturing leadership influence. Yes, you read that right: *essential*.

Recently, largely due to public failures of high-profile leaders (political, business, religious, law enforcement, and military), substantial research and dialogue have emerged regarding leadership effectiveness and longevity. Dr. Robert Clinton, in his groundbreaking article *Listen Up Leaders*, estimated only one-third of all leaders finish well.[1] This data staggers us and begs the question, Why is this so?

Suzy Wetlaufer, in her September 1999 *Harvard Business Review* article, "A Question of Character," raises this inquiry for business leaders.[2] Regardless of sacred or secular perspectives, effective long-term leadership influence and character development intertwine. Both camps also recognize that most formal leadership programs place little emphasis on character development.

A few notable exceptions exist. In his book *The West Point Way of Leadership,* Dr. Larry Donnithorne discusses how the United States' military academies weave character development into officer training.[3] Military leaders execute moral judgments in fluid, rapidly changing, life-and-death situations. Often, highly stressful combat provides little time for reflection. Officers must possess an established "character compass" from which to make these decisions.

> Regardless of sacred or secular perspectives, effective long-term leadership influence and character development intertwine.

In the business world, Dr. Fred Kiel argues for the critical impact of a leader's character in *Return on Character.*[4] His research offers key elements of character development required for long-term business impact and moral decision-making. Mature, responsible leadership requires moral decision-making and so much more. You'll see what I mean as we examine the character stage of the Redemptive Leadership Model.

Exposing the Insidious Side Effect of Success

In the first stage of leadership development, as discussed, our skills and experiences form into competencies. Our influence expands as others recognize our effectiveness. Eventually, we understand the principles behind our competencies, which broadens our leadership influence beyond our formal training. This "leadership intelligence," as coined in the last chapter, forms a way of thinking or a mindset about leadership. Both emotional intelligence and strategic intelligence serve as subtypes of leadership intelligence. The leadership intelligence or principle stage increases and enlarges our influence. Increasingly others seek our wisdom. This success, however, can manifest a dark side.

The Dark Side of Success

Remember Lincoln's quote at the beginning of this chapter? By changing one word I can clarify the point I am making. The adapted quote reads as follows: Nearly all men can withstand adversity, but if you want to test a man's character, give him *success*.

I would change the word *power* to the word *success*. Often the crucible of success exposes the deeper core structures of our lives. Few experiences intoxicate us like being the conquering hero leading a team to success.

Recognition, financial reward, and respect follow. We become the go-to person, the one with the answers. Our influence broadens. Leadership conferences and books are filled with stories of increasing success, the principles leading the way, and the formulas allowing others to do the same. Understandably, when we experience success and recognition, we want more. In fact, success becomes addictive, evoking the desire to doggedly pursue the next big accomplishment. Continued achievements often plant the subtle seeds of arrogance.

The pull for success ripples downward and outward through the organizational system. In time, the senior team experiences the downward pressure to produce the next big accomplishment and a growing dependence on the senior leader's achievements for their own job security and financial reward. Frequently, this evolves into a self-perpetuating pressure, passed to the next circle of leadership. Direct reports to the senior team encounter the same pressure to contribute to their boss's next victory and so on. Like multiplying cells, this DNA replicates outward, creating a toxic organizational culture.

As our achievements mount, we not only shape our own expectations and the expectations of our leadership team but also those of our governance board, stockholders, members, and other stakeholders of the organization. We promote an ever-increasing expectation of a "success mindset."

In my experience as a leadership coach/mentor, senior leaders universally articulate the burden this mindset eventually brings: *I have to hit the ball out of the park each week. I really need a grand slam! My sales goals are higher next year than ever before.* In this mindset, getting a "single" feels like a failure. Leaders carry the weight of more money, larger buildings, more programs, an expanding staff, a new and revised compelling vision, increasingly deeper insights into the Word of God and so on. An organizational culture emerges with the belief, always unspoken, that an upward spiral of success into infinity is not only possible but also essential. Leaders and followers then work harder, longer, faster, and smarter to preserve this belief.

> An organizational culture emerges with the belief, always unspoken, that an upward spiral of success into infinity is not only possible but also essential.

This dynamic fuels the dark side of success. We, as leaders and the people who follow, buy into something we cannot sustain—made all the more insidious by our good and noble goals (like we find in ministry). Achieving these goals, when we achieve them often enough, sets us up to fail eventually. Thus, the very success we pursue has embedded in it the seeds of a growing crisis.

Many pathways lead to this crisis. For some leaders, the unbearable pressure results in burnout, depression, or crushing anxiety. Key staff may resign after feeling used, unappreciated, or treated like a means to an end. Other leaders experience addictions, moral failures, health issues, lapses in ethical judgment, or a cross-gender friendship that crosses the line but never becomes sexual. It may be a spiritual disconnect with God and loss of meaning in work. *Does all the effort really make a lasting difference?* Friends may conduct an "intervention," confronting our disengagement, irritability, and workaholism. Tragically, lonely spouses may reach a tipping point and decide they must leave the marriage. All the pathways to crisis just listed come from the stories of leaders I have coached.

When the crisis hits, it rocks us, rippling into the foundation that we once thought was secure. Like a catastrophic blow to a car windshield, any sense of confidence shatters into a thousand pieces. Moses experienced this type of crisis at the well of Midian.

Crises Can Create Crucibles

Tim liked to work hard. In fact, his work ethic, instilled by his father at an early age, served him well in college and graduate school. After being recruited by a Big Four accounting firm, he passed his CPA exam with flying colors on his first try. No small feat! Quickly he became a rising star at his firm. His billable hours, as well as his income and bonuses, consistently rose. He gained a reputation for resolving difficult cases and was promoted to project leader, then director, and finally partner in the firm. His reputation for being the wonder kid fed his confidence. As a key leader in his company, he progressively took responsibility for his firm's largest and most difficult accounts. He worked extreme hours to meet deadlines in his busy seasons. By all metrics, Tim oozed the qualities of a successful leader in his field.

I met Tim at year sixteen in his career. His hands trembled uncontrollably in our first meeting.

"I don't know what's happening to me," he said emphatically. "I feel like my chest weighs a thousand pounds and I can't sleep. I keep thinking, what if I make a mistake? What if I can't live up to everyone's expectations? What if I let my partners, the people who work for me, and my family down?" The pressure had been building for a while. An unintended dividend of his accomplishments led to endless expectations and, cumulatively, to a breaking point. Tim's body created a crisis in the form of panic attacks, his well of Midian.

Midian's well represents a crucible. Crucibles squeeze us, creating stress fractures that form the core danger *and* key opportunity for this stage of leader formation. I know, I know, this sounds crazy! *How could a key opportunity reside in such mounting pressure?* It's counterintuitive. Much of how God develops us occurs counterintuitively. God's ways, after all, are not our ways. Paradoxically, the crucible of crisis opens a deeper portal into the character stage of leadership development. Here we must face our shadow side.

Forging a Deeper Understanding of Character

Character can be defined in many ways. I will summarize a few common views on character and then explore an expanded understanding.

Typically, we define character as a set of ethical standards or moral beliefs, which govern behavior. As nineteenth-century English historian and statesman Baron Thomas Babington Macauley describes, "The measure of a man's character is what he would do if he knew he never would be found out."[5] Here, character relates to what the person does, regardless of external consequences. The consequences may be others' opinions or the impact of external rewards or punishments (examples: fines or penalties from violating the law). Thus, a person's actions originate from within and not from external influences.

Consider another definition of character by one of the greatest examples of character in American history, Abraham Lincoln: "Character is like a tree and reputation like its shadow. The shadow is what we think of it; the tree is the real thing."[6] Lincoln similarly defines character as something internal to the individual guiding external action. Note, he frames the internal state as the *reality* and the external action as the *shadow*. Often, we think the other way around. We view our actions and our ability to perform and get results as the reality, the objective mattering most. Lincoln says no, what matters most resides deeper inside us. Developing this core, interior place presents uncharted territory for the majority of leaders. Most find it far easier to employ competencies and performance against a quantitative metric. The character and transformation stages of the Redemptive Leadership Model focus on internal core development. Remember our friend Moses sitting by the well of Midian? He points the way for us.

Here's a New (Old) Way of Thinking

> Developing this core, interior place presents uncharted territory for the majority of leaders. Most find it far easier to employ competencies and performance against a quantitative metric.

Now I will focus on the importance of developing a new (old) way of thinking about character. Examine this text with me from Romans 5:3–5 (NASB): "And not only this, but we also exult in our tribulations, knowing that tribulation brings about perseverance; and perseverance, proven *character*; and *character*, hope; and hope does not disappoint, because the love of God has been poured out within our hearts through the Holy Spirit who was given to us" (emphasis added).

The Greek word *dokime*, translated "character," provides a compelling word picture which hints at the meaning of character. The root of this word means "engraved." We've all inspected engravings on jewelry, coins, and monuments. Metal or stone has been cut away or imprinted with a die, resulting in a mark or engraving.

I don't know if you've ever observed the process. I toured a workshop in colonial Williamsburg, Virginia, some years ago. The artisans utilized period techniques and tools from colonial America. One jeweler looked through a magnifying glass and, with a small tool, hand-etched a design onto a pendant. He *engraved* the jewelry. The resultant engraving represented the mark left by the tool, created by the skill of the craftsman. Thus, the Greek word dokime refines our understanding of character. Character can be defined, in my view, as the deep marks left in our core structure, formed by the shaping events of our lives.

Obviously, by this definition we all possess character. We have all been marked by events in our lives, which impact us sometimes in ways we do not fully understand or recognize. They mark us for good *and* for ill. In fact, events usually mark us in both ways.

Sometimes we view our strengths, in excess, as our greatest weaknesses. Thus, confidence (strength) when overused results in an arrogance (weakness), which alienates others. I would say our strengths and weaknesses correlate or correspond with each other, forming two sides of the same coin. Some traditions label the negative side of the coin as our "dark side," or "shadow." I compare it to a photographic negative. In the days before digital photos, film cameras took negative images that produced positive images in the printing process. We could hold the photographic print, or positive image, in our hands and show it to our friends. The negative image displayed the reverse of the print image. Thus, the photographic print and its corresponding negative provides a great analogy for understanding the relationship between our strengths and their shadows.

Let me illustrate further. In order to understand who I am at a core level, you must understand my father's story. My father lost his father in a tragic mining accident just six days before his birth in 1930. My grandmother, a woman with no education, living in a company-owned town in rural West Virginia, lost her husband, the meager income they subsisted on, and her home. Providing for four children through the Great Depression became her constant worry. I can't imagine how overwhelmed my grandmother must have felt. Those circumstances "engraved" themselves on my father's core and later made a residual impact on me in turn.

My father learned to work hard at a very early age. I remember him telling me stories of being picked up at dawn by the milkman when he was only six. Dad ran the bottles of milk to the door from the horse-drawn milk wagon. Working hard grew into a pattern in my father's life. At some deep unspoken level, he always felt poverty breathing down his neck, regardless of his financial condition.

No one spoke about working hard in our family. No one wrote it down on a "core values" list. It wasn't necessary. Hard work was integrated into the culture of our family. This culture marked me—just like my father's life-shaping circumstances engraved themselves on him. As a result, I developed a strong work ethic and capacity, which serves me well in most circumstances. I do not think about working hard or really consciously choose to do so. It emanates from my core; it's who I am. This work ethic drives the acquisition of my leadership competencies. These competencies benefit the people and organizations I serve. My competencies, like the photographic negative, possess a dark side, however.

For most of my life I've struggled with maintaining work-life balance. I can easily and unintentionally neglect my family, my marriage, and my health. I also find it easier to just do things myself rather than ask for help. As a leader, my dark side frequently manifests without me realizing its impact. If I talk about healthy balance as a necessity for leadership longevity, but live another way, I erode my credibility. My example trumps my words no matter how well-reasoned. You see, my strength, my capacity to work hard, possesses a dark side. All of our strengths do.

The Moon Has a Shadow

Mark Twain poignantly observed, "Everyone is a moon, and has a dark side, which he never shows to anybody."[7] This implies the light and the dark form two sides of a whole. You don't get one without the other. I take exception to the last part of Twain's quote suggesting the dark side is never shown. Unlike the dark side of the moon, our shadow always manifests, especially to those whom we live with or lead. For leaders this often occurs in the crucible of success, which I mentioned earlier. Several crucial implications for the character stage of leadership development stem from this observation.

Take a moment to review our foundation. A leader's competency expands influence and, over time, allows the second stage of leadership impact to emerge. I view this as the principle or intelligence stage of leadership, which expands and deepens the leader's influence. This expanded influence catalyzes the crucible effect. The pressure of achievement surfaces the dark or shadow side of an individual's leadership strengths. In fact, this pressure often amplifies the dark side. A good friend framed it this way: "This pressure is like squeezing a tube of toothpaste: what's on the inside starts to come to the outside." Our team, family, and organization experience the ripple of our dark side. A great opportunity lies here, as counterintuitive as it may sound.

> Unlike the dark side of the moon, our shadow always manifests, especially to those whom we live with and lead.

The outcome of Tim's story mentioned earlier in this chapter embodies the counterintuitive opportunity cloaked in his shadow's unveiling. Tim initially viewed his crisis as an ending point. His shattered self-confidence, fractured stamina, and seemingly lost resilience could only result in diminished trust from his employees, fellow partners, and clients. He envisioned a downward spiral culminating in a lost career and financial ruin. In hindsight, his seeming ending became a new beginning. The wake-up call of his distress activated an inward journey to explore the shaping events of his life driving his need for unending accomplishment. Ultimately he articulated and reprioritized his values, gained new skills in establishing personal boundaries, and shifted his mindset about his career. He now advocates and coaches others in his firm to do the same.

Crises Possess a Hidden Potential

Another influential American speaker and author, Helen Keller, once said, "Character cannot be developed in ease and quiet. Only through the experience of trial and suffering can the soul be strengthened, vision cleared, ambition inspired, and success achieved."[8]

Crisis. Don't you love that word as a leader? Not! In fact, we usually view crises as the bane of our existence. Crises absorb tremendous organizational resources, time, and emotional energy, distracting us from strategic objectives. They fill our already jammed schedule with a tsunami of extra meetings. If viewed from a different angle, however, crises possess a hidden potential, opening a pathway to deeper leadership development. I know, I know, this sounds crazy at first blush.

From a Western mindset, we typically view crises as events to avoid or overcome versus opportunities to embrace and harvest. Consider another point of view.

The diagram below depicts the Chinese word for crisis:

The Chinese language, as you may know, utilizes word pictures or ideograms. The word for crisis shown above contains three word pictures.[9]

The left image portrays the Chinese word for danger. Looking closely and using your imagination, it represents a person standing on the edge of a cliff ready to slide off.

If you examine the third image, to the right of the center letters, it sketches the Chinese word for opportunity. Again, with imagination, it represents a chrysalis or cocoon. This middle stage of a metamorphic process characterizes the in-between place where a caterpillar will soon emerge as a butterfly.

The middle ideogram, the circle with a line through it, renders the Chinese word for balance. Thus, taken in its entirety, a rich definition emerges, yielding a very different view of crisis. A crisis represents the balance point, the tipping point, between danger and opportunity, between openness to insight and defensiveness.[10]

Crises has the potential to garner our attention and open our eyes like nothing else. Particularly true for leaders, success tends to impede our self-awareness and cloak our shadow. Nothing intoxicates like good results, by whatever metric. When we bask in the warm sunlight of success and admiration, we become less open to feedback about our personal shadow and growth areas. Crisis, on the other hand, penetrates through our hubris and opens our eyes.

May I ask a sobering question? Think of the highly competent senior leaders in your experience who possess blind (shadow) spots. How often were teammates or family impacted by their shadow issues? Let me pose another question: What impedes a bright, competent leader from confronting self-limiting shadow issues? A leader's success often insulates them from the feedback they need. We've all heard statements like "You can't argue with results," "Don't be a part of the problem, be a part of the solution," or "Focus on the positive, don't nitpick the negative." Honest feedback recedes in the face of these responses. Honestly, at times I've said these things in the face of

criticism from others. Usually I've done so with a bit of
sophistication, saying, "I'll take that into consideration."
Regardless, teammates and family decipher the message
that I'm reluctant to accept criticism.

So, what can penetrate through our success defenses
and potentially catalyze our growth and maturity as
leaders? Crisis! Crisis is
revelatory, opening our
eyes in an unequaled man-
ner. The crisis may be of
our own making like a
significant failure. Pastor
Joel's moral failure from the introduction fits this category.
In other circumstances, another person's failure ripples
outward touching our lives with unanticipated impact. A
family member's illness, an abrupt financial downturn, or
a sudden marital issue may also open our eyes. A thousand
paths lead to this place of crisis. The question becomes,
Will we embrace the opportunity by opening our eyes and
continue looking? Will we harvest the learning necessary
to take us to another place?

> Particularly true for leaders, success tends to impede our self-awareness and cloak our shadow.

James 1:22–24 captures this notion well: "But prove
yourselves doers of the word, and not merely hearers
who delude themselves. For if anyone is a hearer of the
word and not a doer, he is like a man who looks at his
natural face in a mirror; for *once* he has looked at himself
and gone away, he has immediately forgotten what kind
of person he was." James cautions us to avoid personal

and leadership self-delusion (hiding behind successes and competency) in order to find a place of clear vision. We must not "delude" ourselves. Instead James exhorts us to penetrate our delusion by facing our "natural face in a mirror," thus cultivating self-awareness. By implication, the mirrors of other people's feedback and, in this case, the Scriptures expose our blind spots. James admonishes us not to avoid personal (and I would say leadership) amnesia. Avoid being the person who "has immediately forgotten what kind of person he was." Thus, we must continue to look deeply into ourselves. This constitutes the inward journey of the character stage of leadership development.

Again, Moses' life illustrates the pattern expressed so far in the stages of the Redemptive Leadership Model as follows. For the initial forty years of his life, he cultivated the competencies and principles of leadership, which served him well in the later years of his journey. Growing up as a prince of Egypt, Moses' education likely consisted of the best Egypt could offer. We know that Egypt, in this period of ancient history, possessed advanced knowledge in art, astronomy, mathematics, medicine, science, written language, engineering, logistics, and the military arts. Reasonably, we can assume Moses' grooming, as a member of the royal family, had given him commensurate experience and prepared him for a leadership role.

Some historians speculate he had led troops in battle as a commander. As a seasoned leader, when Moses issued

the call for the Hebrews to rise up and follow him, I think
he fully expected the people to recognize his prowess as
a leader and follow. Events took an unexpected turn for
Moses, however.

When Moses sat down at the well of Midian, it
marked both a crisis point and a turning point. Little did
Moses know, the burning bush lay forty years in his future.
Forty years! The crisis symbolized by the well of Midian
launched an inward journey of character development
for Moses. The years between the well of Midian and the
burning bush marked Moses; they changed him. The man
who sat down at the well of Midian differed intrinsically
from the man who encountered the burning bush.
Unknowingly for Moses, this journey opened his eyes and
prepared him for the next stage of leadership influence.

The Character Stage Presents Several Dangers

In my experience, several dangers of this stage warrant
consideration. Typically, highly competent leaders do not
wait well. Studies document their bias toward action. In
most settings, taking action serves them well and helps
accomplish critical objectives.

Brent's story typifies the unintentional cloaking by-
product of success. Brent demonstrated superior leadership
gifting. Most initiatives he touched exploded with
growth. His start-up organization grew from a handful
to several thousand members with nearly unprecedented
acceleration. Recognition and broad influence resulted.

Most were blindsided when his secret life became public, resulting in a failed marriage, questions about his character, and his governance board firing him. Brent's entrance into the crisis stage was like a speeding automobile publicly slamming into an immovable object. It got everyone's attention. It was revelatory.

Encountering the character stage presents three distinct dangers:

1. The Rebound Effect—Leaders tend to view the initial crisis of this stage as a "speed bump," or anomaly, laser-focusing on fixing the problem as quickly as possible. They reach for their tried and true competencies, working harder, smarter, and longer in an attempt to power through the crisis. Supporters and anyone else who depends on the leader will aid and abed this tendency with encouragement—"get back in the saddle," "don't get distracted," "stay focused"—in order to exercise the stewardship of their gifting. Brent was encouraged as offers poured in asking him to lead new start-ups. Though well-intentioned, his peers suggested exercising his leadership gifts would allow him to move on rather than get bogged down in self-doubt. The draw of being wanted and feeling purposeful became irresistible.

Counterintuitively for a leader, the inner
work of this stage must not be fast-
tracked. Fast-tracking leads to the second
danger.

2. The Groundhog Day Effect—Getting back
    in the saddle, even if too soon, initially feels
    great! It creates a sense of security, and the
    leader begins to receive the old accolades as
    a result of flexing their competencies. They
    laser-focus with improved performance,
    and insidiously the old pressure builds
    again. In my experience the cycle time
    to the next crisis shortens. Leaders may
    change jobs, move locations, change
    ministry types, change marriages, and hire
    a new senior team only so many times
    before facing themselves at a deeper level.
    The amnesia eventually wears off, and they
    remember the image in the mirror from
    the first time around. Brent encountered
    the Groundhog Day effect firsthand. He
    told me, upon reflection, that his rushing
    the process set him up for his next crisis.
    He threw himself into his leadership role
    in a new organization with great vigor.
    After all, he had even more to prove after
    his first failure. His workaholism and drive
    for results blinded him from seeing how

he lost the trust of his senior team. After a mass exodus of key thought leaders, his governance board again fired him. Shaken and disoriented, he returned to his well of Midian.

3. The Derailing Effect—A major danger of this stage involves losing our way as leaders. After experiencing repeated crises with shorter cycle times, leaders often become discouraged and disillusioned, and begin pulling away from the known and familiar. Especially true for ministry leaders, they find themselves losing motivation for the life purpose they once felt called to. Some feel hurt, abandoned, and betrayed by God and those in their organizations. The quicksand of jadedness and bitterness exerts gravitational pull. Tragically, when experienced leaders disappear, they never see their story redeemed. The discouragement and bitterness radiated from Brent when I met him sometime after his second termination. Withdrawn and sober, he had pulled away from his former circle of friends and colleagues. His defensiveness betrayed the woundedness he carried from his last termination. For the first time in his life, Brent could not find his way. Fortunately

for Brent, he reengaged an inward journey
to deconstruct his protective walls. A
number of leaders do not. They harden
their defenses and become entrenched in
old patterns.

This Stage Builds Humility While Preparing Us for Greater Influence

The character stage shifts the locus of leadership
influence from our competencies and understanding
of principles to something much deeper inside of us.
Some consider this the breaking process portrayed in the
biographies of Scripture. Joseph, Moses, Peter, and Paul
all illustrate this paradigm. Their stories demonstrate the
linkage between a crisis moment, their well of Midian, if
you will, and the inner cultivation of heart humility, which
leads to unforeseen amplified influence. Our competence
and effectiveness, representing the first two stages of our
model, rarely cultivate humility in us. Success, a heady
thing, bolsters our sense of self-importance and significance,
especially when others tell us how able we are. Ironically,
this insulates us from and expands our blind spots or
shadow.

I believe the character stage has several purposes:
1. To teach us the insidious danger of relying
    solely on our competencies and successes
2. To open our eyes to the linkage between
    our competencies and their corresponding

dark side. We then seize the opportunity to peer intentionally into our blind spots, confronting our shadow.

3. To cultivate awareness of our need for God and others, opening a window for increased relational vulnerability

4. To cultivate readiness to enter the transformation stage of leadership development

Moses provides a compelling archetype of both the pattern and potential of this stage. The forty-year-old capable prince of Egypt entered through the portal of his failure. Little did he know, arriving at the well of Midian would become a defining moment changing him forever. From our perspective, we know the man who encountered the burning bush some forty years later was internally different. Forty years later? Clearly, Moses did not fast-track the process! Instead of rushing, he spent many hours reflecting on the circumstances, motives, and decisions leading him to a place of seeming barrenness. He looked deeply into the mirror of his own life. Moses did not attempt this process alone. His father-in-law, Jethro, became both a companion and advisor to Moses. He remained so throughout the rest of Moses' life (see Exodus 18).

Moses' well of Midian marked the gateway to a period of brokenness which led him to a deep internal yieldedness. He no longer trusted his competencies alone but came to depend on God at a qualitatively different level. These shifts led him to a place of readiness to encounter God through a burning bush (Exodus 3:2). The burning bush heralded the greatest period of Moses' leadership influence.

Can Leaders Skip the Character Stage?

Often, when I teach the Redemptive Leadership Model, someone will ask, "Do you mean all leaders *must* experience crisis or failure in order to deepen their leadership influence?" Usually, the person asking stands squarely in the competency stage or the principle/ intelligence stage. The question reflects the underlying belief that if you know enough and work hard enough, you can avoid crisis points and failures.

The irony of this question highlights the point of the character stage. This stage dismantles the illusion that we control our own destinies. With experience, we realize so much occurs beyond our control. We finger the scar tissue from our last unanticipated crisis and think, *How could I ever think I was so invulnerable?*

As we enter the character stage from the principle/ intelligence stage, we ask the questions of "How long will this last?", "How fast can I recover?", and "How much can I still accomplish?" As we move into the breaking process of the character stage, we ask a different set of questions, reflecting a different mindset: *What is the condition of my heart?*; *What really matters?*; and *What is most meaningful?* In this stage and the next, beliefs become convictions. Abstract knowledge moves into experiential reality. Let us turn our attention to the next stage of leadership development, the transformation stage.

Chapter 3 Reflection Questions

1. Reflect on the following quote: "Regardless of sacred or secular perspectives, effective long-term leadership influence and character development intertwine." Why do you think this is such a critical concept when considering leadership influence?

2. This chapter explored the idea that success has a shadow side. What do you think of this concept, and how have you experienced this in organizations you've been a part of?

3. Identify your own well of Midian, and record the story of how it formed you.

4. Consider identifying some of the shadows of your leadership strengths.

5. What are your takeaways from this chapter?

CHAPTER 4

THE TRANSFORMATIONAL LEADER: A CHANGE OF HEART

*Be at least as interested in what goes on inside you
as what happens outside. If you get the inside right,
the outside will fall into place.*

—Unknown

Getting at the heart of transformation proves to be no easy task, primarily because transformation involves an inward work of the heart, which then works its way outward into our thoughts, behavior, and mindset. Through transformation we become different at our core and then cannot help but think and behave differently. Consequently, transformation cannot be defined by a series of steps or practices. In this chapter we'll explore the heart of transformation by examining the word itself as well as transformational stories of real people (biblical and otherwise) who illustrate the process. Please consider each story in this light: *What does this vignette tell me about transformation?*

Trevor always seemed to know what to do. Friends and acquaintances viewed him as highly competent, self-assured, and extraordinarily disciplined. A big fish in a medium-sized pond, his influence touched the majority of those living in his city. National leaders sought his advice and attempted to recruit him for their organizations.

Upon reflection, Trevor later verbalized, he sensed turbulence in his interior world. Something was missing that he couldn't identify. Though immensely effective in his job, his restlessness resulted in a decision to begin developing pastors behind the so-called Iron Curtain. This new sphere of influence required hard work, courage, and considerable vision. Trevor possessed these qualities in spades. As you might guess, his efforts resulted in a growing sphere of influence. Here, in the midst of this new success, Trevor arrived at his own well of Midian through a moral failure. This crisis blindsided and shocked him. It did so for all who knew him. I met Trevor in the midst of this turning point. Disoriented, broken, scared, and reeling described him in our first encounter. He thought, given his old paradigm, he was finished as a leader. Little did he know his greatest leadership influence lay ahead. Little did he know a portal had opened to the transformation stage of his leadership development.

The crisis of the character stage, when embraced, garners our attention as nothing else can. It opens our eyes. It strips any illusion of self-sufficiency and sets in

motion the process of brokenness, which can lead to yieldedness. Yieldedness, when cultivated, forms the soil of humility from which deeper, more grounded influence germinates. This process is the focus of this chapter. Nichole
Nordeman, in her song "The Unmaking" (2015, Birdwing
Music), captures this tip-
ping point when she
describes the crumbling of
our walls of self-sufficiency
opening to a period of
deep reflection and evalua-
tion.

> The crisis of the character stage, when embraced, garners our attention as nothing else can.

Biblical Biographies Inform Us about Transformation

Consider the many people in Scripture (Hebrews
11) whose lives deeply and radically changed. We've talked
a lot about Moses, who went from being the prince of
Egypt to the most humble man on the face of the earth—
and emerged more powerful, godly, and influential for the
change. The well of Midian marked an essential waypoint
on his leadership journey.

Then there's Peter. Forceful and impassioned,
he reached his well of Midian in a moment of fear and
despair, leading to his disavowal of Jesus—something
Peter, like our friend Trevor, swore he would never do. He
became the denier, wracked with grief, as the realization
of his failure sank in. Jesus, in a profound moment of
forgiveness and redemption, renamed him. The Betrayer

became the Rock, foreshadowing the radical shift in who Peter would become. Peter's crisis and subsequent transformation resulted in a man who spoke fearlessly in the face of opposition and personal threats.

Thousands became followers of the Way through their encounters with Peter. His first sermon concludes with the charge, "Repent, and each of you be baptized in the name of Jesus Christ for the forgiveness of your sins . . . . For the promise is for you and your children and for all who are far off" (Acts 2:38–39). He spoke with such authority and power! What made him so believable? Clearly, Peter knew firsthand what it meant to be "far off," needing to be brought near through grace and forgiveness. He knew it in his bones. It irrevocably transformed him, and he emerged a different man.

Saul of Tarsus took pride in his religious background, education, and dedication. All with good reason, he excelled at being a Pharisee, one of a Jewish sect that defined the concept of knowing the right thing and doing it. His competencies and focus were incontrovertible, and he marshaled his fervor against followers of Jesus, attempting to destroy their new movement.

Remarkably, just a few years later, this same man devoted his life to the very church he persecuted. How did this radical change happen? Saul encountered a crisis, which brought him to his own well of Median. Remember, crises come in countless forms. Act 9:1–19 chronicles this moment for Saul. In the midst of drivenness and

clarity of purpose, destroying the Way, he experienced a
Jesus moment that completely derailed him. Suddenly,
everything that gave meaning to his life crumbled,
and he recognized his blindness both literally and
figuratively.

I can't imagine the magnitude of disorientation,
grief, and brokenness for Saul. This crisis opened a
transformational portal for him. At the beginning of Acts
9, Saul "breath[ed] threats and murder against the disciples
of the Lord" (v. 1), but by verse 18 he gained spiritual sight
(and physical sight, too), realigning his life as a follower of
the Way. (Remember that crises, when engaged, opens our
eyes.) Saul, the murderer and persecutor, transformed into
Paul, the messenger of grace, hope, and love. Paul never
recovered from this crisis; it changed him forever. In fact,
it transformed his core.

Transformational stories fill the Bible's pages.
Abram, who doubted, became Abraham the archetype
of faith. David, a murderer and adulterer, remained the
symbol of a man after God's own heart (Acts 13:22).
Jacob, the deceiver, became Israel, the man who displayed
God's work in his life through his limp. Again and again
we observe radical, core-level shifts in men and women,
depicting the transformational process.

These accounts trigger skepticism in some of
us, mostly because we rarely observe this kind of
transformation in our day-to-day lives, resulting in the
conventional wisdom that people don't really change

much. Maybe you've succeeded in breaking a bad habit or noticed a coworker turning up the heat to meet a performance goal. Admittedly, these efforts make a positive life impact. However, tweaking our game or following through on a New Year's resolution doesn't qualify for most of us as fundamental transformation. Yes, we can change things about ourselves, but do we *really* change at our foundations, and if so, how? Paul wrestled with this question. Before examining his thoughts, I want to explore a few underlying frameworks of how we tend to view change.

Change Involves More Than What You Know

My college years represented a time of significant spiritual growth. Involved in a campus ministry, I wanted to progress in my faith and help others do the same. Without consciously knowing it, I began to adopt a model, or framework, for change. Influenced by two mentors, I embraced several practices in order to mature spiritually. One of these, memorizing Bible verses, grew into a meaningful habit for me. I used the Topical Memory System developed by the Navigator organization and still possess stacks of business-card-size verses from that period.

A second practice I learned involved using the Inductive Bible Study method developed by a gentleman named Irving Jensen. In addition, I used a prayer journal, joined a small accountability group, and looked for opportunities to serve others. These practices provided invaluable structure that supported my spiritual growth at the time and still pay dividends today.

Stepping back, I now recognize the framework I assimilated. Simply put, it goes something like this: Learn the right information (knowledge), work to align your behavior to that knowledge (obedience), ingrain the behaviors through repetition (habits). At the time, I believed this framework captured *the* biblical structure for change.

I based my position on Paul's statement in Romans 12:2: "And do not be conformed to this world, but *be transformed by the renewing of your mind*, so that you may prove what the will of God is, that which is good and acceptable and perfect" (emphasis added). How do we become transformed? By renewing our minds, of course. What could that mean? At the time, as stated, it meant acquiring the right information (truth) plus a healthy dose of self-discipline. Sound familiar?

This model of change underlies much of our Western mindset. Books abound applying it to marriage, faith, leadership, personal, and organizational growth. It usually presents as a version of *The Five Steps (*or *Principles* or *Secrets* or *Habits) to Improve Your (fill in the blank with Marriage, Finances, Faith, Church, Organization, or Sex Life).*

In my doctoral training in psychology, professors termed this change model "cognitive-behaviorism." Hard data from extensive research demonstrates this approach benefits everything from personal growth goals to overcoming depression and addiction. In terms of faith development, I clearly prefer

> I am fully convinced a cognitive-behavioral framework cannot explain biblical transformation.

knowledge to ignorance and mature habits to bad behavior. In all areas of life, informed action plans and clear behavioral goals provide excellent focus and productive traction. For all its value, however, does cognitive-behaviorism adequately capture the essence of biblical transformation? Contrary to my earlier beliefs, I am fully convinced a cognitive-behavioral framework cannot explain biblical transformation. Let me unpack this statement.

Seeing True Transformation Shifted My Framework for Change

Early in my experience as an urban pastor, the passion to understand how people change was ignited in me. For more than thirty years, I have been privileged to work with thousands of individuals, couples, leaders, seminary professors, pastors, and organizations all expressing the desire to change. My education, but mostly my experience with real people, led me to this observation: If knowledge really catalyzed deep change, then seminary professors, seminary students, and informed Christian leaders would exude profound transformation and Christlikeness. But just like the experts in Jesus' day (the Pharisees), knowledgeable believers often miss the deep change Jesus taught.

When we attempt to achieve transformation through cognitive-behavioral therapy, we practice what a friend calls "The Gospel of Knowledge and Duty." Know the right things and do the right things. The transformation Jesus taught and the examples of Abraham, Moses, David, Peter, and Paul speak to a deeper, core heart shift. Don't get me wrong: there's nothing wrong with knowledge or duty . . . unless we mistake them for transformation.

My postdoctoral residency at the Minirth-Meier Clinic in the mid-1980s drove home the necessity to transcend the Gospel of Knowledge and Duty. The clinic, an early pioneer in faith-based treatment, attracted believers from across the nation and some from other countries. Often these men and women sought help in addressing problems they had wrestled with for years but still experienced feeling stuck in them. Typically these individuals, frequently seminary or Bible college graduates, were experienced in church life and often led churches or ministries. They exhibited the discipline, determination, sacrifice and competency to succeed in their work/ministry lives. Acquiring in-depth biblical knowledge, they worked hard to apply it to their behavior. Yet, they longed for a deeper level of change, which continued to elude them. Why? Because deep change—transformation—does not come about by obtaining knowledge, biblical or otherwise, and modifying behavior alone.

Unknowingly, most sincere believers, including leaders, have adopted the Gospel of Knowledge and Duty. It often leaves us feeling like failures, unqualified to lead, and creates a pressure to hide our ongoing struggles. I can't tell you how often I continue to hear (after over thirty-plus years now) some version of this story from lay people and Christian leaders alike. The true stories of women and men longing for more confronted me, compelling me to reevaluate my framework for change.

A Deeper Look at Transformational Change

As I stated earlier in this chapter, the Bible presents many rich stories of radical, transformational change. The New Testament Greek word for transformation, *metamorphoo,* marks an important starting place to deepen our understanding. The word appears only four times in Scripture (emphasis added below):

And He was *transfigured* before them; and His face shone like the sun, and His garments became as white as light. (Matthew 17:2)

Six days later, Jesus took with Him Peter and James and John and brought them up on a high mountain by themselves. And He was *transfigured* before them; and His garments became radiant and exceedingly white, as no launderer on earth can whiten them. (Mark 9:2–3)

But we all, with unveiled face, beholding as in a mirror the glory of the Lord, are being *transformed* into the same image from glory to glory, just as from the Lord, the Spirit. (2 Corinthians 3:18)

And do not be conformed to this world, but be *transformed* by the renewing of your mind, so that you may prove what the will of God is, that which is good and acceptable and perfect. (Romans 12:2)

Even a cursory examination of these verses offers important insights. Usage of the word *transformation* in these passages from Matthew, Mark, Romans, and 2 Corinthians cannot be reduced to a linear, structured, cognitive-behavioral process. The first two passages offer a vignette of the deity of Christ revealed through His human form. This moment provides an echo of the presence of God revealed to Moses during the giving of the Ten Commandments. The 2 Corinthians passage carries the same sense and weight. Clearly, these three texts link transformation to a supernatural event linked to an encounter with the person of God Himself. Encountering God transforms us. This poignantly informs our framework of transformation.

Our English word *metamorphosis* comes from the Greek word *metamorphoo*. The second part of this compound word, morphosis, carries the meaning "to change."[1] We use a shortened form of this word, morph, to describe how computer-generated images in films change form. In the *Avenger* movie series, Dr. Bruce Banner morphs into the Incredible Hulk. He becomes more than a bigger, faster Bruce Banner. He morphs into something entirely different. The first part of the compound word, meta, indicates a structural change of form. Together, they give us the sense of metamorphosis.

As an example of this kind of change we often refer to the changing of a caterpillar into a butterfly. As you know, a butterfly does not represent just an improved caterpillar—a caterpillar with more legs or one that is stronger or faster or has more disciplined behavior. No, a butterfly becomes fundamentally different from a caterpillar. It has changed, or metamorphosed, at an essential level.

True Transformation Changes Us at Our Core

Have you ever encountered someone who experienced a very close brush with death? Tina, a bright, educated, successful, and highly capable consultant, illustrates the impact of this kind of event. As the result of a routine medical exam, she discovered she had stage II cancer. She commonly worked sixty-hour weeks and traveled a great deal speaking to audiences across the country.

The diagnosis clarified things for Tina. She stated that it changed her. In fact, it changed everything from how she ate, how much she worked, how she viewed her relationships, what she did with her money, and how she prioritized her time. She refused to postpone the important things any longer. Actually, the crisis of the diagnosis transformed her as she processed its meaning. Tina lived in the world with a different frame of reference because she became a different person. It became her well of Median.

> True transformation changes us at the core. It's like shedding our old skin and creating something radically new.

True transformation does that: it changes us at the core. It's like shedding our old skin and creating something radically new. Jesus described it as getting both new wine and a new wine skin. By implication, it's a shift on the inside as well as the outside.

Part of the reason we reduce transformation to an exercise in cognitive-behavioral management results from a misunderstanding of Romans 12:2. Just like I did early in my faith walk, we take the English word *mind* to refer only to the informational cognitive process. The Greek word *nous* does mean "mind," but it means much more than the processing of information. In Matthew 22:37, Jesus says this: "You shall love the Lord your God with all your *heart*, and with all your *soul*, and with all your *mind*" (emphasis added). Quoting from Deuteronomy 6, Jesus uses heart, soul, and mind to describe the core or essence of a person. The terms are used in a holistic way to describe a person's core. Thus, the word *mind* does not refer to cognitive processes alone any more than the term *heart* refers to emotions alone.

In Jesus' Day, Both Heart and Mind Referred to Our Essence

In Western culture we tend to dichotomize heart and mind, so we talk about either emotions or thinking. No such division existed in first-century Palestine. Both the heart and the mind in Jewish life refers to the core of our being, our essence. In a discussion about defilement, Jesus illustrates this by saying,

> Biblically, the heart refers to the seat or essence of our personhood.

"But the things that proceed *out of the mouth* come *from the heart*, and those defile the man. For out of the *heart* come *evil thoughts*, murders, adulteries, fornications, thefts, false witnesses, slanders" (Matthew 15:18–19, emphasis added). You see how Jesus links the heart and thoughts and behavior? He considers them as a whole, not discrete compartments. Thus, the heart and mind both refer to our emotions, but more than our emotions, to our behavior, but more even than our behavior. Think the whole package: emotions, thoughts, will, intentions, behavior. Biblically, the heart refers to the seat or essence of our personhood.

Digging deeper, Paul, in the 2 Corinthians 3:18 text, paints a vibrant picture of the nature and depth of transformation. Writing to this community of believers, he earlier sets the context in 2 Corinthians 3:2–3 by saying, "You are our letter, written in our hearts, known and read by all men; being manifested that you are a letter of Christ, cared for by us, *written not with ink, but with the Spirit* of the living God, *not on tablets of stone*, but on *tablets of human hearts*" (emphasis added). Paul powerfully contrasts the image of tablets of stone with tablets of human hearts. The difference couldn't be more important or stark, as he makes clear in verse 6, where he says we are "servants of a new covenant, not of the letter, but of the Spirit; for the letter kills, but the Spirit gives life."

Paul states the tablets of stone, the law given to Moses, produce death. I believe this frames the Gospel of Knowledge and Duty. The new covenant (v. 6) points another way. He develops the image of Spirit-heart writing, which brings vibrancy and life. The human heart, our core, becomes the locus of this Spirit work.

Paul sets the stage for his conclusion in verse 18 by referencing Moses and the veil (see Exodus 34:29–35).

As you may remember, exposure to God's presence on the mountain made Moses' face radiant. As the glory of God faded from Moses' face, he wore a veil to conceal the fading process. Paul takes these rich images and pivots them, pouring expanded meaning into them, and applying them to the heart and mind: "But their *minds were hardened*; for until this very day at the reading of the old covenant the same *veil remains unlifted*, because it is removed in Christ. But to this day whenever Moses is read, *a veil lies over their heart*" (2 Corinthians 3:14–15, emphasis added). Though not the focus of our current discussion, I wonder what factors "harden" and "veil" us, or block us, from accessing heart transformation. Paul then summits his argument in verse 18 by saying: "But we all, with *unveiled face*, beholding as in a mirror the glory of the Lord, are *being transformed* into the same image from glory to glory, just as from the Lord, the Spirit" (emphasis added).

Look closely with me at several key elements of this verse. The *unveiled face* mentioned here contrasts with the veiled face or hearts discussed earlier. The Greek word used here, *anakalypto*, means to uncover or to "unhide."[2] I believe hiding, which naturally results from the Gospel of Knowledge and Duty, blocks transformational process. Unveiling our face—exposure, unfiltered honesty, and authenticity—activates it. The phrase "being transformed" indicates that metamorphosing operates in an ongoing and progressive way; it's not a single event. And transformed

into what? The very "image" of the Lord that we behold
"as in a mirror."

Theologians call this the *Imago Dei*, Latin for the
image of God. This harkens back to our original creation,
in Genesis, as image bearers. Catch the thrust of what Paul
says: unveiled exposure to
the nature and person of
God through His Spirit
metamorphoses us. This
exposure changes our core
molecular structure, if you
will, so that we begin to
radiate His image. What
Paul explains here cannot
be viewed as a cognitive-behavioral adjustment. While we
may be tempted to turn Romans 12:1–2 into a cognitive
formula, this verse (2 Corinthians 3:18) defines
transformation in a way that defies natural explanation.
Transformation, like regeneration, must be viewed as
fundamentally supernatural, requiring the intervention of
God through His Spirit. To catch this vision requires we
abandon our simple formulas, drop to our knees, and
glorify our Creator.

> Transformation,
> like regeneration,
> must be viewed
> as fundamentally
> supernatural, requiring
> the intervention of God
> through His Spirit.

God Needs a Partner in Your Transformation: YOU!

You might ask at this point, *If transformation requires
the supernatural work of God's Spirit, do we play any part in
the process, and if so, how?* Absolutely! Tina, whose story

we introduced earlier, illustrates the point. When her well of Midian occurred, she could have doubled down on her busy life to avoid dealing with her own mortality. Instead, she allowed her health crisis to catalyze deeper change in her.

You see, although we need the supernatural work of the Spirit to do the transforming, we can resist or distract from the very events that open these windows of opportunity. Like Tina, Saul of Tarsus or Peter could have done the same. Each could have aborted the process. King Saul of the Old Testament illustrates the contrast in resisting transformational windows in his life. Samuel, his mentor, confronted his tendency to take action based on his own competency. Saul's jealousy of David, offering a sacrifice without Samuel, and the inner turmoil he chronically experienced all reflect the condition of his heart. King Saul repeatedly hardened his heart or entrenched his defenses. He aborted the opportunity for heart change.

James 1:2–4 provides foundational insight into the pattern of transformation. I believe it describes a high-view outline of the process. It reads, "Consider it all joy, my brethren, when you encounter various trials, knowing that the testing of your faith produces endurance. And let endurance have its perfect result, so that you may be perfect and complete, lacking in nothing." These verses map the stories of many biblical characters and our own: transformation is essentially linked to trials. In fact, James encourages us to consider it joy when we face them—not

because we enjoy them but because of the potential they
hold for deep change. Note, we do not plan for trials or
manufacture them; they just come, all on their own. If we
pump blood, breathe air, and rub shoulders with people,
trials will come. Our task, if we desire transformation,
means facing trails with a different framework. The very
framework James provides.

The Greek word James uses for trials (*peirasmos*)
refers to testing the character of a thing. You may test the
genuineness of a substance by taking a core sample, by
piercing it or conducting a biopsy. Similarly, trials pierce
us assessing our inner condition. This dynamic occurs in
every hero story from classical literature to current films.
In the midst of adversity (trials), the hero must face some
essential aspect of himself or herself.

Films like *The Lord of the Rings* and *Star Wars* illustrate
the point. Gandalf, in the mines of Moriah, stands alone
and faces his greatest foe in mortal battle. Luke Skywalker,
training as a Jedi, enters the cave in which he must face
his dark side and battle against it. Abraham must face a
crisis of faith related to God's promise of an heir. Jacob
must face a brother he betrayed after deceiving his father-
in-law. David must face the murder of Uriah, the adultery
with Bathsheba, and the loss of his child. Peter must face
his betrayal of Jesus, and Paul his spiritual blindness, self-
righteousness and cruelty.

Each of these trials drilled a core sample into
the heart of the individual, exposing . . . unveiling . . .

something essential that must be faced. This crucible effect commonly brings us to the end of our self-sufficiency and self-importance. When not aborted, individuals emerge from the crucible profoundly different and transformed.

As the crucible effect builds, we must endure, which James provides in the second part of his transformational outline. The Greek word *hypomone*, used in James 1:3–4, provides a rich image. Literally it means to "stay under."[3] Visualize pressure building in the crucible, providing an opportunity for piercing and transformation or the choice to abort it. For me, the desire to escape the pressure, or fast-track the process, comes reflexively. If we abort the process too early, we often short-circuit transformation. It's like following a recipe but taking the dish out of the oven too early or cutting open a chrysalis before the butterfly becomes fully formed.

You Can't Rush the Process

I am privileged to work with leaders from across the country and some from across the globe. Most contact me at the point of their greatest crisis. Highly competent, bright, and impactful, these men and women face some form of crisis of James 1 proportions. They find themselves in the pressure of the crucible. It may be some form of damaged relationship, conflict with a governance board, marital distress, moral failure, burnout, a major transition, or past woundedness that creates the crisis. I meet with the person or the couple in what I call Leadership Intensives, which involve fifteen to thirty hours of face-to-face exploration and development.

Patrick, one of those exceptionally gifted leaders, got in touch with me through a mutual friend. He could walk into a room of strangers and, in a relatively short amount of time, people would look to him for advice or guidance. He projected a winsome confidence and sincerity. An entrepreneur, Patrick could identify opportunities and draw people together to make things happen.

Some years before our meeting, Patrick planted a church in an affluent area with influential people from across the country. The church flourished, reaching a group of individuals whose names most would recognize. In the midst of his ministry flourishing, as often occurs with leaders, his deeper shadow side began to surface. His drive and high capacity for accomplishing important tasks left his marriage strained and his family vulnerable.

One day, his spouse sat him down and told him she didn't like who he had become. She felt uncertain if she wanted to be married to him. Patrick's devastation radiated from his eyes as he verbalized feeling blindsided by his wife's revelation. Patrick stated he wanted to "do whatever it takes" to win his wife's trust. He asked me about the goals of the Leadership Intensive, how the process would work, what the key indicators of progress would be, what homework would be assigned, and when to include his spouse.

Unintentionally, he began marshaling his competencies, making his wife a "project" to be completed. Paula, as you might guess, wanted nothing to do with this approach. She stated, "Patrick just doesn't get it; he hasn't for a long time. He's missing the point." Paula nailed it. Patrick missed the point.

Most accomplishment-oriented people, like Patrick, want to ask the question they, at some level, know not to verbalize out loud: *How long will it take before things can get back to normal and I can resume my work?* Toward the end of our first meeting I said to Patrick, "I know you want to ask me a question but haven't put it on the table yet. I'm going to answer it anyway. *How long will this process take?* As long as it takes for you to stop asking that question." You see, I began confronting something deeper in Patrick. He required a shift in his framework. Paula longed to be more than a project to him, and as long as she "smelled" Patrick approaching her that way, her wounds would not heal.

Understandably, Patrick wanted to fast-track transformation. But to be truly transformed by our trials requires moving beyond asking "How quickly can I recover from this?" to believing "God will use this crucible to deeply form His image in me." When trials squeeze us for the sake of trans-

> When trials squeeze us for the sake of transformation, speed or quickness misses the point.

formation, speed or quickness misses the point. The point must be deep engagement with God metamorphosing our core.

When we stay engaged and let endurance finish its work, James says, we become "perfect and complete, lacking in nothing." Talk about transformation. I love how James repeats himself, three times no less, so that the impact won't be lost: the process cultivates wholeness and maturity. Encountering the trials allows a core character sample to be revealed, and engaging the crucible forges deeper wholeness and maturity. We become authentically more like Christ.

The Greek word James uses for "complete," *holokleros*, sheds some light on his meaning. It references the practice of breaking a stick into small pieces of equal size. One shorter stick is added but held with the rest of the sticks so they look like they're the same length. Then people are allowed to draw sticks, but no one wants to draw the "short stick." "Complete" refers to the "whole stick," with no part missing. James frames the transformational process as creating wholeness in the sense of nothing essential being missing. God, through the transformational process, desires to complete us according to His original design.

James frames the end result of the transformational process as "lacking in nothing." That's different from how we usually grow, isn't it? We tend to find our strengths and settle into them, content to maximize their development while other parts go unattended, or at least underutilized. It would be the equivalent of going to the gym and only doing the exercises we already excel at. But that's a far cry from "lacking in nothing." James encourages us toward symmetrical development. In cycles, the process of James 1 exerts a kind of pressure highlighting and developing our weaker side, not just our strengths.

Patrick experienced this effect. Through a series of circumstances, he and Paula decided to leave their affluent community and prestigious position to become a host couple in a home where traveling VIP Christian speakers stayed. One night their house provided a reception for a well-known Christian leader. Patrick told me the story of walking to the curb, garbage bags in hand, after cleaning up from the event. He looked up at the sky that night and reflected on his journey.

A year before, he would have been the VIP leader doing the speaking, or at least the emcee introducing him. "I never dreamed that year would be so difficult," he told me. That night at the curb, under the stars, he reaffirmed to God his commitment to "stay under," to stay engaged in the transformational process. He gradually recognized his need to slow down and confront the old attitudes of self-sufficiency, self-importance, and arrogance. He began to see Paula not as a project but as a person. Paula experienced the difference. She saw a greater sense of humility and servanthood in Patrick. This heart transformation drew her to him.

Today Patrick pastors a small church outside New York City. He influences key leaders on Wall Street, conducting Bible studies with diplomats from the United Nations. Patrick's competencies, personality, and gift mix clearly contribute to his current ministry impact, like they did when I first met him. The difference resides on the inside. His heart, or core, has changed. Patrick's competencies might have aborted his James 1 process if he had chosen the quick fix and bounced back into ministry. Relying solely on competencies at the potential expense of transforming his heart would have made Patrick miss God's greater point: developing Patrick's redemptive influence and message.

Three Concerns about Transformation

The power of the transformational process, an important effect of the gospel, nevertheless presents several concerns. Consider the following:

1. We can become overly mired in our inward focus. Transformation requires a journey inward, but nearsightedness and self-focus may unintentionally result. Granted, keeping perspective between too much external focus versus too much internal focus requires judgment to navigate. This leads to our next caution.

2. We should not try to go it alone. While no one can take the transformational journey

for us, at key inflection points we all need wisdom from those who have traveled before us. Maintaining perspective is not a solo activity. Moses needed Jethro, David needed Nathan, and Paul needed Barnabas.

3. We may turn our experience into a formula. As explored in James 1 and other passages, transformational principles operate in a variety of circumstances. Each person's trial possesses a unique flavor and becomes the entry point for a distinct transformational journey. Insightfully, Paul invites readers to imitate his life but not formulize it. Imagine the absurdity of a book based on Paul's example:

Five Steps To Transforming Your Life
Chapter 1: Go Blind
Chapter 2: Get Stoned and Left For Dead
Chapter 3: Get Shipwrecked
Chapter 4: Get Bitten By a Poisonous Snake
Chapter 5: Languish in Prison

4. We may develop an insidious attitude of elitism. Unfortunately, we naturally think in terms of a better than/less than paradigm. When we experience the value resulting from our trails, emerging with greater

depth, we can subtly view earlier stages as "less than." Paradoxically, this attitude sprouts an upside-down form of arrogance. *Once you experience more brokenness, then your impact will increase.* We must take care not to undermine those in other stages of development.

The Purpose of This Stage: To Help Others

The old axiom "We teach what we know, we reproduce who we are" captures a key learning of this stage. As leaders and disciples, we must actively experience transformation, that we might catalyze and guide the transformation of others. When we stay engaged with God and others in the midst of *our* trials, they shape *us*. When we stay engaged with God and *others* in the midst of *their* trials, we serve as transformational guides. Our own transformational process develops the wisdom to see transformational windows opening in other people's journeys.

Henri Nouwen's book *In the Name of Jesus* describes individuals who journeyed into the desert (literally) desiring to encounter God deeply.[4] These "Desert Fathers" left the comfortable and familiar, entering an austere foreign environment. In the midst of this disruption, they wrote about encountering God at a profound, heart-transforming level. I wonder what "squeezed" them? What created the "crucible effect"?

Perhaps living in such a disorienting environment, or the absence of family and friends, or the intensity of such a small inter-dependent, unconventional group, or the silence. How often, I wonder, did they want to escape and get out from under the crucible? Some remained for decades.

Nouwen observes that their experience was remarkable upon returning from the desert. They lived in the world in a different way. People now experienced these individuals as being centered, humble, grounded, loving, focused on the welfare of others and particularly the marginalized. They became more like Jesus and others experienced more of His Image in them, thus the book title *In the Name of Jesus*.

So, do we need to sell all and move into a monastic community in the desert? No!! Remember, formulaic thinking misses the point. Many paths lead us to the crisis which becomes a transformational window. Our choice becomes, will we "stay under," engaging the process, or abort it? The resulting deep, structural heart transformation allows us to live and lead from a different place. We do not, as leaders, abandon our competencies or understanding of principles, but others experience the difference inside us. I believe this heart shift generates a deep level of credibility to speak hope into people's lives, which we will now explore in the next chapter involving the redemption stage.

Chapter 4 Reflection Questions

1. Reflect on a particular crisis point in your own life. How did this experience initially impact you? Retrospectively, how did it open a transformational portal in your life?

2. Interact with this quote: "These accounts trigger skepticism in some of us, mostly because we rarely observe this kind of transformation in our day-to-day lives, resulting in the conventional wisdom that people don't really change much." Do you agree or disagree? Why or why not?

3. In your experience, how have brokenness and humility been linked?

4. What is your takeaway from this chapter?

CHAPTER 5

THE REDEMPTIVE LEADER: UNLEASHING THE HEART AND CATALYZING HOPE

Brokenness to redemption, where mercy and grace kiss both sides of our face. Brokenness where we are split open, redemption where God knits us back together.

—*Lysa Terkeurst*

THE THIEF BREATHES FREEDOM, but his heart remains imprisoned. Thievery had defined Jean Valjean; he stole for necessity and then habit. Rarely shown mercy or love, he was shocked when a well-meaning priest offered food and shelter. Living out of his true nature, Jean Valjean tramples the goodwill of the priest by assaulting the Monseigneur and stealing all the silver he finds. Why do his actions baffle us? After nineteen years in chains for stealing food when young and hungry, he expressed the criminal identity ingrained in him. When caught the next morning by the authorities, he is returned to the only man who has ever shown him kindness. Valjean, resigned and hardened, knows what lies ahead: another sentence in hell. At least he assumes.

"I'm sorry to disturb you, Bishop Myriel," the officer says. "I've had my eye on this man and we searched his knapsack and found all of this silver." Laughingly he states, "He claims you gave it to him!"

"Yes, of course I gave him the silver," replies the priest.

Disorientation washes over the gendarmes, the housekeeper, and most of all Valjean. The surprises continue to unfold. "Madame Ghiello," the bishop instructs, "Fetch the silver candlesticks." He chides Valjean, "Why did you leave them behind, Jean Valjean? They are worth at least two thousand francs!"

Blinking uncomprehendingly, Valjean watches as the gendarme removes the shackles from his wrists, then the soldiers retire to the house for wine.

The Monseigneur approaches Valjean, removing his hood. His gaze penetrates Valjean's soul. Valjean's discomfort becomes palpable.

"Why are you doing this?" he stammers.

"Don't ever forget, Jean Valjean, my brother, you no longer belong to evil. With this silver I bought your soul. I've ransomed you from fear and hatred. Now I give you back to God."[1]

The encounter became an inflection point for Valjean. It disoriented him, marked him, and ultimately transformed him.

This poignant scene from the film version of Victor Hugo's *Les Miserables* provides entrance to our conversation regarding redemption. How can we understand the essence of redemption? Why do stories of redemption inspire us? How does redemption inform our leadership paradigm? These questions shape this chapter's focus.

Les Miserable highlights redemption's nature while demonstrating the force of redemptive influence. Bishop Myriel views Jean Valjean through different eyes. He senses potential below the surface narrative, obscured to everyone else. The priest fades from Hugo's story, but his redemptive influence marked Valjean for the rest of his life. It started here, the moment of the redemptive tipping point.

Exploring the Counterintuitive Nature of Redemption

At first glance, in Valjean's case redemptive influence seems absurd, even illogical. The night before, the monseigneur had been struck by Valjean when he interrupted the robbery. The priest received a beating from Valjean; why would he now shower the thief with gifts? Why would he gift not only silverware but candlesticks as well, all in the aftermath of unjust treatment? By inference, we gain significant insight into the bishop. His unexpected actions bewilder all present. I wonder what shaping events in the priest's own story prepared him for this moment with Valjean. What cultivated his ability to see moments like this through such a different framework?

Redemption operates under a different logic—a deeper kind of logic—a spiritual logic. Fundamentally, counterintuitive, redemptive expressions demonstrate radical love. To experience redemption at work requires faith-vision, viewing life events as infused with a greater purpose. Faith-vision discerns a deeper narrative in the stories swirling around us.

The priest, perceiving a redemptive turning point in Jean Valjean's life, did the radically unexpected thing. The immeasurable impact was to astonish a criminal to the point he could never recover. It changed the course of his life because it transformed his core. The priest saw the deeper narrative of Jean Valjean's life. Inspector Javert, by contrast in Hugo's story, could only see the surface criminal narrative of Valjean's life.

Only in God's logic does it make sense to pay those who want to take your life with the gift of life. In the priest we hear echoes of Jesus' teachings to turn the other cheek when struck and give away your coat when your shirt is taken.

> Fundamentally, counterintuitive, redemptive expressions demonstrate radical love.

Bishop Myriel lavishes Valjean with gifts in the same way God lavishes love on broken people. Redemption, so near the heart of God and so intrinsic to His nature, is most clearly seen in Jesus' life, death, and resurrection. Redemption must not be viewed as just an event but as a different paradigm, a different operating system, based on God's heart.

Redemptive Encounters Are Discovered in Unexpected Situations

In 1993, sixteen-year-old Oshea Israel shot and killed Mary Johnson's only son, Laramiun. While Oshea sat in prison, Mary struggled with deep roots of bitterness that incapacitated her life and affected her relationships.

A dozen years later, knowing she needed a change, she decided to visit the young man who murdered her son. When they met at Stillwater Prison in Minnesota, the two shook hands.

"I don't know you and you don't know me," she explained. "You didn't know my son and he didn't know you, so we need to lay down a foundation and get to know one another."

To Mary's surprise, Oshea wasn't like the hardened sixteen-year-old she witnessed in the courtroom. He was a grown man who admitted what he had done and he asked for her forgiveness.

Two hours later they said good-bye, and the two hugged. Walking out of the prison visiting room she thought, *I just hugged the man who murdered my son.* Instantly, all the anger and the animosity stuffed deep in her heart over the previous twelve years dissipated. She knew she had completely forgiven him.

Eventually after his release, Oshea moved next door to Mary. Because her biological son is no longer alive, she treats Oshea as her son. Because Laramiun never graduated from college, she told Oshea, "Now you're going to college."

They've even shared the incomprehensible words "I love you."

And Mary calls him "son."

(You can listen to an interview of Mary and Oshea at www.storycorps.org.[2])

Mary Johnson changed operating systems. She, like the priest in Hugo's *Les Miserables*, began looking below the surface narrative of Oshea's life. A compelling shift ensued which led to a redemptive encounter . . . for both of them.

In some ways, this chapter is the most difficult to write. Simply parsing the word *redemption* or providing examples cannot fully communicate its depth. While true of other stages, only by sitting on the receiving end of redemption can we adequately understand its power. Nevertheless, examining the framework of redemption in Scripture helps establish categories for our discussion.

We Must Understand the Essence of Redemption

The notion of redemption occurs early in the book of Genesis with the promise of deliverance (Genesis 3:15) and weaves its way through the biblical narrative concluding with John's Revelation. Some would say the scarlet thread of redemption runs through each biography and all sixty-six books of the Bible. Biblically, no person lives beyond redemption's reach.

The centrality of the tabernacle and temple highlights God's redemptive purpose for the nation of Israel. The sacrifices, scapegoat, veil, ark of the covenant, mercy seat, and intercession of the high priest on the Day of Atonement all point to His redemptive framework and His redemptive heart toward His people.

The stories of Adam, Eve, Abraham, Isaac, Jacob, and Moses exemplify personal redemption. David, in his psalm of repentance, Psalm 51, possesses keen insight into the personal, inward elements of redemption. In verses 16–17 he says, "For You do not delight in sacrifice, otherwise I would give it; You are not pleased with burnt offering. The sacrifices of God are a broken spirit; A broken and a contrite heart, O God, You will not despise."

Redemption, David says, focuses on the heart, our interior world, and thrives in the cultivated soil of brokenness. An inward redemptive journey transforms a person's core (discussed in our last chapter), which results in a profound framework shift. We begin to see with different eyes.

Remember how the priest believed the deeper narrative of Jean Valjean? Remember how Mary Johnson came to see the deeper narrative of Oshea Israel? David, a man after God's own heart (Acts 13:22), received the gift of redemption and came to view the world and people through a different lens.

The New Testament deepens our understanding of redemption by focusing on Jesus' life. Early in Luke, Anna, a prophetess, encounters baby Jesus at the temple with his family. We read in Luke 2:38, "At that very moment she came up and began giving thanks to God, and continued to speak of [Jesus] to all those

> Redemption, David says, focuses on the heart, our interior world, and thrives in the cultivated soil of brokenness.

who were looking for the *redemption of Jerusalem*" (ephasis added). This corporate redemption (Jerusalem, the nation, and God's people in general) later expands to emphasize other forms of redemption:

- **Individual redemption.** "Being justified as a gift by His grace through the redemption which is in Christ Jesus" (Romans 3:24).
- **Physiological redemption.** "We ourselves groan within ourselves, waiting eagerly for our adoption as sons, the redemption of our body" (Romans 8:23).
- **Future focus of redemption.** "Then they will see the Son of Man coming in a cloud . . . . lift up your heads, because your redemption is drawing near" (Luke 21:27–28).

The New Testament's scope and reach of redemption's influence create a seismic impact with profound implications.

The New Testament Greek word for redemption, *apolytrosis,* possesses multiple nuances of meaning.[3] The first, paying a ransom, captures a sense of the first-century slave markets. Conquering armies sold their prisoners into slavery. Redeeming a captive involved purchasing or paying a ransom.

A second nuance of redemption involves being liberated, released, and set free. In this sense the captive was not only purchased but also liberated. The Greek word's emphasis on freedom includes literal freedom, as in breaking chains, but also carries the meaning of unbinding bandages, releasing from a burden or affliction, being forgiven, and emancipation.

Biblically, redemption thus carries the force of breaking the chains binding us and catalyzing an inflection point of vitality and hope. The broken chains may be external or internal. This framework of redemption involves far more than the forgiveness of sins. Redemption, embodied by Jesus, encompasses freedom, empowerment, vibrancy, and alignment with God's heart and purposes. As Randy Alcorn, author and professor, writes, "Jesus' miracles provide us with a sample of the meaning of redemption: a freeing of creation from the shackles of sin and evil and reinstatement of creaturely living as intended by God."[4]

The priest in *Les Miserables*, through this lens, exemplifies a redemptive leader: "With this silver I've bought your soul. I've ransomed you from fear and hatred. Now I give you back to God." The man's actions result in not just Valjean being spared another prison sentence, nor in him just being allowed to go as a free man. This redemptive act entirely charts a new course in Valjean's life, freeing him to live as he has never imagined. Marked by this moment, Valjean becomes an agent of redemptive influence touching others' lives through the rest of Hugo's story.

Redemption, a love word, expresses the heart and nature of God toward us and His vision for us. Redemption embodies a person (Jesus), an act (the cross), and the means of unleashing our redemptive influence.

Barnabas Modeled Redemptive Leadership

Let's turn to another redemptive leader: Barnabas. Not as well-known as many early church leaders, Barnabas repeatedly met people at key turning points, catalyzing their redemptive potential. We meet Barnabas early in the book of Acts: "Now Joseph, a Levite of Cyprian birth, who was also called Barnabas by the apostles (which translated means Son of Encouragement), and who owned a tract of land, sold it and brought the money and laid it at the apostles' feet" (Acts 4:36–37).

Acts 4 gives initial insight into Barnabas' character and reputation. Born Joseph, the Apostles renamed him Son of Encouragement for good reason. Here and later in

Acts, we observe his pattern of becoming aware of a need and stepping forward to meet it. In this case, he contributes financial and no doubt emotional support to people at a critical juncture in their faith. The Son of Encouragement sets a poignant example in the early church's formation.

The next vignette of Barnabas occurs at a pivotal moment in the life of Saul of Tarsus and the young church. You will remember Saul persecuted the followers of Jesus, putting many to death, including Stephen in Acts 7. After his conversion, Paul traveled to Jerusalem seeking to meet the church's leadership. "When [Paul] came to Jerusalem, he was trying to associate with the disciples; but they were all afraid of him, not believing that he was a disciple" (Acts 9:26).

You can appreciate the apostles' position. Earlier, Saul considered his mission to extinguish the Way, putting men and women to death. Would not such a man feign conversion in order to expose the church's leadership, or worse? The apostles simply did not believe him.

Imagine Paul's experience. Your world, turned upside down by a revelatory crisis, exposes how off course you really are. Can you identify with Paul? Most of us can. Then, those wounded by and disappointed in our actions pull away, rightly, in self-protection. Eroded trust and credibility leave our words and promises meaningless. What do you do when others can't believe you? In situations like this, we need an advocate who, redemptively, recognizes the deeper narrative. Enter Barnabas.

Barnabas viewed Paul differently. Acts 9:27 states, "But Barnabas took hold of him and brought him to the apostles and described to them how he had seen the Lord on the road, and that He had talked to him, and how at Damascus he had spoken out boldly in the name of Jesus."

Here Barnabas, like the bishop in *Les Miserables,* takes a man written off by others and says, "I believe in him." I love how the text says Barnabas *took hold* of Paul and *brought* him before the apostles. Have you ever needed for someone to come, find you, take hold of you, and bring you along? Barnabas perceived a redemptive moment the apostles did not. This Pharisee, now a follower of the Way, demonstrated the power of God to transform the heart and unleash a redemptive message. The persecutor became the preacher.

No doubt Barnabas recognized Paul's intelligence, training, and passion, which were considerable, but he recognized something more. If a man self-described as "a blasphemer and a persecutor and a violent aggressor" (1 Timothy 1:13) could be so radically transformed, no one exceeds the grasp of grace. Barnabas understood God would speak through Paul *because* of his story, not *in spite* of it. That's what a redemptive leader does: they recognize the potential, not just

> Have you ever needed for someone to come, find you, take hold of you, and bring you along?

in a person's giftedness but in their struggle and dark side. In fact, this became central to Paul's message: "It is a trustworthy statement, deserving full acceptance, that Christ Jesus came into the world to save sinners, among who I am the foremost of all. Yet for this reason I found mercy, so that in me as the foremost, Jesus Christ might demonstrate His perfect patience as an example for those who would believe in Him for eternal life" (1 Timothy 1:15–16).

Paul wasn't the last person Barnabas invested in despite opposition from others. Later, Barnabas chose to work with another emerging leader—despite opposition from Paul: "Barnabas wanted to take John, called Mark, along with them also. But Paul kept insisting that they should not take him along who had deserted them in Pamphylia and had not gone with them to the work. And there occurred such a sharp disagreement that they separated from one another, and Barnabas took Mark with him and sailed away to Cyprus. But Paul chose Silas and left, being committed by the brethren to the grace of the Lord" (Acts 15:37–40). Understanding the background to this conflict sets the stage for grasping its meaning. Mark had deserted Paul and Barnabas on a previous missionary endeavor. John Mark's disappointing failure impacted Paul so strongly that he rejected him for the impending journey. Barnabas took an equally strong but opposite position. Barnabas and Paul's history and previous ministry relationship frame the significance of this conflict.

What compelled Barnabas to advocate so resolutely for John Mark? What did Barnabas see in him? We don't know exactly. We do know while others saw Mark through the lens of his failure, Barnabas perceived the redemptive potential in Mark's life. And he acted on what he saw. He "took Mark with him and sailed away," much in the way he took hold of Paul and brought him along in the past.

Redemptive leaders exhibit this essential quality: discernment, informed by faith, which allows them to view God at work, even in circumstances most would call failure. Don't misunderstand—Barnabas was no fool. He did not champion others out of a fondness for the underdog. Rather, he viewed people through a different optic. He believed leadership development involved more than keeping a perfect track record.

> Redemptive leaders exhibit this essential quality: discernment, informed by faith, which allows them to view God at work, even in circumstances most would call failure.

Because we know little about Barnabas' early life, we can only speculate how he acquired this redemptive discernment. I am confident the Son of Encouragement possessed his own stories of failure, brokenness, and redemption. When we, as leaders, experience our redemptive influence rising from the ashes of our own brokenness, we gain the ability to see the same potential in others. Even when they cannot see it for themselves.

In the case of John Mark, others eventually came to agree with Barnabas' assessment of him—mostly notably Paul. Toward the end of Paul's ministry, in his second imprisonment and probably close to his martyrdom, he made a request of his protégé, Timothy: "Only Luke is with me. Pick up Mark and bring him with you, for he is useful to me for service" (2 Timothy 4:11). Yes, Mark, as in John Mark. The same man Paul excluded from his team because Mark had let him down. Paul now recognized a transformation in Mark and asked for him.

And to think, John Mark's story might have ended with his rejection by Paul in Acts 15. Instead, Mark's influence flourished because a redemptive leader, Barnabas, took hold of him like the priest took hold of the criminal Valjean. When Paul refused to work with Mark, Barnabas discerned an opportunity to redemptively develop a person, just as he had done with Paul. For Barnabas, more was at stake than past disappointments and failures. Today we experience the impact of Barnabas' investment in Mark's life through the gospel bearing his name. The gospel of Mark provides one of the earliest accounts of Jesus' life and ministry and offers testimony to the impact of a redemptive leader at a pivotal moment in John Mark's life.

Redemptive leaders catalyze hope. Why do I say this? Because redemptive leaders truly believe that moments of crisis and failure bear the seeds of a person's greatest influence. Yes, these moments must be embraced and guided well to bear the fruit of redemptive influence. The strenuous efforts of the character and transformation stages are integral to this outcome. Why do redemptive leaders possess such a counterintuitive mindset? In my experience, it can only be forged by the anvil and hammer of our own crises and failures. David Brooks, in his 2015 book *The Road to Character,* gets at this idea when he states, "Success leads to the greatest failure, which is pride. Failure leads to the greatest success, which is humility and learning."[5]

Remember, all leaders value competencies, but what about when our competencies fail? Every leader champions recruiting and developing the best and brightest, but what about when they fail? Redemption is not merely picking yourself up when you fall and starting over. It's not even about succeeding in the face of obstacles. God, as we turn toward Him, shapes meaning and purpose out of our ashes and brokenness. We discover God declares His redemptive nature by working through us *because of,* not *in spite of,* our sin, our dark sides, and our failures. As Paul says in 2 Corinthians 12:9, "And He has said to me, 'My grace is sufficient for you, for power is perfected in weakness.' Most gladly, therefore, I will rather boast ⌐about my weaknesses, so that the power of Christ may dwell in me."

This provides hope for us all.

Why Do Stories of Redemption Inspire Us

Stories of redemption resonate deeply within us. Hugo's Jean Valjean, Moses, Mary Johnson, King David, the woman at the well, Paul the apostle, John Mark, and Peter, the pebble, rising transformed by his failure and renamed the Rock, all bear witness to this harmonic. In fact, redemptive themes find broad expression in art, film, literature, and biography because of their magnetism—characteristically depicted by the archetype of a protagonist rising to a place of "success" and then encountering crisis and failure, which opens the portal to an inward journey. The protagonist then rises from the ashes not healed but transformed.

I believe stories of redemption stir us for numerous reasons. Foremost, each of us bears the imprint of personal suffering and failure. We yearn for crisis events to incubate meaning and purpose and not signal an end to our influence.

Secondly, redemptive stories underscore that we each, without exception, possess shadows. Confronting our shadows requires unveiling our shadows. Observing others who courageously face their personal brokenness encourages us to do the same.

Thirdly, I believe that fundamentally human beings hunger for relationships and life in general to work as they "should." I encounter this craving regularly with my clients in my counseling practice. Often without knowing it, people express what theologians term the Imago Dei, or image of God within them. Our core self (imago) longs to experience all things, including ourselves, redeemed (unleashed, emancipated, vibrant). Redemptive stories oscillate the Imago Dei within us.

Finally, redemptive stories inspire hope. We all need hope—hope that our lives are inscribed with a deeper meaning even in moments of crisis and suffering. The compelling lesson of these stories affirms that, with redemptive guidance, crisis moments hold the potential to mature our core self. The events themselves then transform into symbols marking the shift within us, like Jacob and his limp (Genesis 32:31).

> The compelling lesson of these stories affirms that, with redemptive guidance, crisis moments hold the potential to mature our core self.

David Brooks, in *The Road to Character*, captures the essence of this when he states, "Each phase of this experience has left a residue on such a person's soul. The experience has reshaped their inner core and given it great coherence, solidity, and weight."[6]

What We Learn from Rod Cooper's Story

I met Rod as a graduate fellow in our clinical psychology program in Portland, Oregon. After completing a masters of theology degree at Dallas Seminary, he decided to pursue his PhD in psychology. He and I hit it off right away and became fast friends, thought partners, and eventually true brothers.

Rod began public speaking in his early adolescent years and obtained advanced training in homiletics during seminary. In fact, he won prestigious preaching awards and accolades from leaders across the country and once spoke at a men's stadium event of nearly seventy thousand people. A gifted speaker, he communicates with clarity, passion, and conviction. In the thirty years I've known Rod, the footprint of his leadership influence has steadily expanded. Yet, unknown to many, Rod experiences a great deal of performance anxiety before speaking. Paradoxically, as his leadership influence grew, so did his apprehension. I'm not talking about the normal jitters that most speakers experience before taking the stage. I am talking about paralyzing dread.

"I feel like a catastrophe always lurks around the next corner," he once told me. "I know it's not logical but it grips me." For Rod, this became his well of Midian. Rod began an inward quest to find the source of this fear.

"I remember the strong hands of my dad praying with me like it was yesterday. His labor as a farmer built his muscles, his determination, and his faith. I know he believed in me and sacrificed to ensure that I would have the higher education that remained beyond my dad's reach."

Rod knew when he headed off to college that he had a lot riding on his young shoulders: the weight of his father's and family's hopes and dreams. As a young African-American man, he felt the pressure to succeed. "I know my drive to achieve was fueled by a desire to honor my father's sacrifice."

In college Rod hit a new stride. He did well academically, performed in a prestigious marching band, and expanded his world beyond the small farming community in which he grew up. Each time he returned home to visit, he sensed the weight his father carried on his shoulders. "I knew my dad was worried. Worried about the farm, worried about the crops, worried about the weather, and worried about providing for his family."

The day everything changed etched itself in Rod's memory. "A call came from my family explaining Dad had taken his life. I was stunned and grief stricken. In that instant, my world turned upside down. I had just lost the man I most admired and respected." Rod was now fatherless.

This event, a turning point for Rod, impacted him more than he could possibly understand at the time. "I now know this event marked me with the belief that some unforeseen trauma could strike at any moment. Although I didn't fully know it at the time, I lost a sense of security and well-being in the world." So now, despite a PhD in clinical psychology, a ThM from a well-respected seminary, and success as an admired professor, he was experiencing a deep sense of insecurity. "I know it doesn't make logical sense, but when triggered, this fear overtakes me and I feel one step away from a catastrophe." Through the difficult work of the transformation stage, Rod discovered the root of his anxiety.

Rod's struggle has forged a profound redemptive influence. Even though Rod possesses exemplary credentials and experience, he exudes an openness, approachability, and authenticity instead of arrogance. He serves as a confidant and redemptive guide to many national leaders at their own wells of Midian. Over many years of conversations and coteaching, Rod has helped shape my thoughts about redemptive influence that are presented in this chapter. His influence results *from* his struggle, not *in spite* of it.

What allows a leader, at critical inflection points, to embrace the arduous journey of transformation? One leader, when asked this question, poignantly noted, "It has a lot to do with the genuineness of your brokenness. Genuine brokenness is progressive like a series of stairs. The descent to one level opens your awareness of your own woundedness and how you have wounded others. The Holy Spirit opens our eyes to the next level of what we must face. Genuine brokenness can only be certified by others in the person's life." The redemptive leader's voice offers hope, *because* of their journey, to those at their own well of Midian.

How Does Redemption Inform Our Leadership Paradigm?

A grasp of the redemptive framework, first in ourselves and then in others, shifts our paradigm of leadership development. Cultivating our competencies no longer defines the summit of leadership. Rather, a redemptive framework expands our understanding to view the inward development of the heart as the true pinnacle. Focusing solely on external success at any cost shifts to the recognition that transformational windows commonly open through crisis and often failure. When engaged well, the twin spades of brokenness and repentance cultivate the heart.

This distinct mindset differentiates the redemptive stage of leadership. Redemptive leaders, like Barnabas, recognize opportunity in the crisis points of others' lives, guiding them to discover and unleash the power of their own redemptive stories. These stories, then, multiply redemptive influence by one life touching another, like Barnabas' impact multiplied through Paul and John Mark. Transcending competency alone, the weight of their effect emerges from who they are, not just what they do or know. In *The Road to Character*, David Brooks offers this description fitting of a redemptive leader:

> Redemptive leaders, like Barnabas, recognize opportunity in the crisis points of others' lives, guiding them to discover and unleash the power of their own redemptive stories.

Occasionally, even today, you come across certain people who seem to possess an impressive inner cohesion. They are not leading fragmented, scattershot lives. They have achieved inner integration. They are calm, settled, and rooted. They are not blown off course by storms. They don't crumble in adversity. Their minds are consistent and their hearts are dependable. Their virtues are not the blooming virtues you see in smart college students; they are the ripening virtues you see in people who have lived a little and have learned from joy and pain.[7]

Imagine for a moment you're Jamie from our first chapter, wondering if you're damaged goods. Or you're Pastor Joel after everything blew up, thinking it's unimaginable you could ever lead again. What would it be like if a mature impactful leader came alongside you and believed in you? What if this leader shared a similar background of failings? Can you imagine the hope that would germinate in the soil of your heart? You just might believe—or believe again—that something powerfully redemptive resides in you waiting to be unleashed. Redemptive leaders impart hope. Hope that a deeper narrative really exists to the surface story of our lives. Hope that God is really for us and uses even the broken pieces of our lives to glorify Himself. Hope that God works through broken people.

What Is the Purpose of This Stage?

The redemption stage of the Redemptive Leadership Model reorients a leader outward from the inward journey of transformation. Our focus shifts from confronting ourselves (obviously this is ongoing) to encouraging and serving others from a place of deep humility and wisdom. Deeply marked by our own experience with grace and radical love, we become redemptive voices guiding others to discover their own redemptive narratives.

Luke 22:31–32 provides insight into the dynamic of becoming a redemptive influence in others' lives. Jesus said, "Simon, Simon, behold, Satan has demanded permission to sift you like wheat; but I have prayed for you, that your faith may not fail; and you, when once you have turned again, strengthen your brothers." Obviously, he was referring to Peter's thrice denial after Jesus' arrest, which occurred a few hours later. Jesus knew of Peter's upcoming failure, felt compassion for him, and pointed him toward a redemptive outcome. Interestingly, Jesus said Peter would strengthen his brothers *because* he went through the transformational/redemptive journey. I believe this vignette demonstrates the power of a redemptive leader (Jesus) guiding a person (Peter) at a critical moment because he saw the deeper spiritual narrative at work in Peter's life. Peter never recovered from this encounter.

Instead, he arose transformed becoming an authoritative redemptive voice in the early church's formation.

What Are the Cautions of the Redemption Stage?

Several cautions require consideration in this stage. First, remember that these stages are not formulaic. What constitutes a crisis must always be defined in the context of an individual's life. It may be financial, relational, a conflict, job-related, sexual, the loss of a loved one, or a health issue. The critical idea is that it creates a tipping point, a well of Midian experience.

Second, we must guard against an insidious attitude of superiority or inferiority taking root. Viewing this stage as better than others gives fertile ground for arrogance to breed. This stage's fruit demonstrates humility, not pride.

Third, remember, we do not leave our competencies or leadership intelligence behind. Instead, we incorporate and transcend them in this stage.

Fourth, in hearing this model, people will sometimes ask, "Since redemptive influence rises from our failures, shouldn't we fail all the more so that our influence increases?" Of course not! Paul similarly, in Romans 6:1–2, addresses the question of whether we should sin all the more so that grace may increase. He says essentially this misses the point. Redemption does not diminish the rippling consequences and pain of our failures in our own and others' lives. Redemption does address the deeper narrative of God at work to bring something good and important even out of these tragedies.

Fifth, the emergence of our redemptive influence cannot be rushed or forced. In my experience, leaders possess a natural desire to take action and fast-track most undertakings. Leaders must guard against the belief that we can power our way to redemptive influence. Self-deception leaves each of us vulnerable to the fraudulent conclusion that we have faced our shadows and completed our work. Only wise individuals who know us well can validate the deeper heart change required for redemptive influence. The redemptive journey demands patience and not speed.

In the next chapter I will zoom out to reflect on the Redemptive Leadership Model as a whole and consider its value for individual leaders and their organizations.

Chapter 5 Reflection Questions

1. Reflect on this quote: "Fundamentally, counterintuitive, redemptive expressions demonstrate radical love." Identify a redemptive moment in your own life. How did this moment impact you?

2. What does the following quote mean to you? "Redemption, David says, focuses on the heart, our interior world, and thrives in the cultivated soil of brokenness."

3. How does the discussion of Barnabas as a redemptive leader impact you? Can you identify a redemptive leader or person of influence in your own life? Tell the story of their impact.

4. How does your understanding of redemptive influence your leadership paradigm?

5. What is your takeaway from this chapter?

CHAPTER 6

REDEMPTIVE LEADERSHIP: SUMMARY AND IMPLICATIONS

Sometimes with
the bones of the black
sticks left when the fire
has gone out

Someone has written
something new
in the ashes
of your life.

—*David Whyte*[1]

My thoughts about leadership, expressed in this book, developed over many years. I wanted this work to be practical and accessible and not academic or theoretical. I hope it provides a resource for individuals, teams, and organizations to engage in a different conversation about leadership. In order to do so, I believe we must use a different framework for the discussion. Generally, most leadership models view competency as the summit of leadership development. The Redemptive Leadership

144

Model views competency as only the beginning stage, necessary and important but only the entry point in understanding leadership influence.

This model seeks to reorient our leadership mindset and values. Instead of the most prized characteristics of a leader being competence, toughness, a focus solely on external success, aggressiveness, invulnerability, intimidation, and "never letting others see you sweat," this model focuses on the brokenness necessary to cultivate the heart and germinate humility. By contrast, the lack of internal development for seasoned leaders often germinates hubris, which becomes their limiting factor. The task of internal development, in the second half of a leader's life, contrasts with the skill development focus of the first half. The Redemptive Leadership Model also views crisis and failure through a different optic. Instead of an ending, this model views them as a portal to go deeper. Leaders with enough mileage, life experience, and scar tissue may reach the wisdom of the redemption stage of leadership.

> Redemptive Leadership Model also views crisis and failure through a different optic. Instead of an ending, this model views them as a portal to go deeper.

What Inspired the Development of This Model?

The Redemptive Leadership Model originated from experience. My work as a psychologist, leadership coach, and leadership professor has allowed me entrance into the lives of thousands of men and women leaders for over three decades, often in moments of vulnerability, crisis, and failure. Frequently, I am privileged to follow an individual's journey over months or years. As a result, I have observed redemptive stories repeatedly rise from brokenness. Observing this pattern hundreds of times shifted my thinking regarding God's development of leaders.

This model is also grounded in the study of leader biographies presented in Scripture. I have unpacked a few of these in earlier chapters. An unmistakable and prevailing pattern emerges: God uses broken people. This understanding of redemption as the dominant theme in Scripture affords us an interpretive lens that highlights God's heart toward us. He delights in redeeming all aspects of our lives, including our crises and failures.

For over fifteen years I have taught some version of this model. This includes doctoral classes with experienced leaders, church teams, business leaders, and individuals at the crisis points in their lives. I have taught it to men and women as well as emerging leaders, existing leaders, and re-emerging leaders. Consistently, a deep and positive resonance occurs. In my judgment, this confirms the hunger leaders possess for something more than traditional competency approaches to leadership development. This book results from the many requests for a work framing the Redemptive Leadership Model.

How Bob Impacted an Entire Class of Experienced Leaders

I met Bob in one of the early doctor of ministry cohorts at Gordon-Conwell Theological Seminary. Dr. Rod Cooper and I had developed the Redemptive Leadership curriculum for the program and cotaught the classes. We asked each student to create a graphic time line of key life events and then plot five high points and five crisis events or failures from their life journeys. We did this so students would get to know each other and to lay a foundation for applying the Redemptive Leadership Model to each student's life. Bob, a seasoned leader in his midsixties, shared the following story in class.

"I grew up in a very poor neighborhood in South Boston. Everyone was poor, so I really didn't have a contrast. The first major crisis in my life occurred when my dad abandoned our family. We went from being poor to barely surviving. My uneducated mom eked out a very meager living for our family; times were very hard then, with not enough food and little else."

Bob then told us about the day his mom gathered his siblings and him into a cab for a ride to a place outside the city.

"We were all excited!" he said. "We had never ridden in a cab, much less been outside of our neighborhood. Eventually we pulled into a driveway that led to what looked like a mansion."

"My mom said to us, 'Kids get out of the car and sit quietly on the steps while I go inside.'"

"After a bit, she came back out and got into the waiting cab without saying a word and drove away."

Bob described a man in a suit who said to them, "Kids, come inside. This will be your new home."

"We were so confused," Bob stated. "It took us awhile to realize we had been taken to an orphanage because Mom couldn't support us."

Bob eventually began to work in the kitchen. The head cook, George, showed kindness to Bob and became the first man to mentor him.

"For two years that relationship was great. For the first time an adult taught me about life. I learned how to work hard, how to prepare food, and how to read a recipe. I loved it."

Then, Bob remembered when things turned. "George, after several years, began to sexually abuse me. I never told anyone because I wanted so badly to please him." This continued until Bob turned eighteen and left the orphanage.

Bob did not have a place to live, so he joined the army. After boot camp his first assignment was a military base in South Korea. "I loved being in the army," Bob said. "It gave me a sense of pride and built my self-esteem. I developed really good friends." There in South Korea, Bob met an army chaplain who introduced him to faith and began to disciple him. The chaplain so impacted Bob that he decided to attend Bible college when he finished his enlistment.

Just before Christmas of his first semester, the academic dean called Bob to his office. "I remember being very nervous entering his office and sitting down across the desk from him."

"I have reviewed your academic performance," the dean said, "and have concluded you don't have what it takes to succeed here. You will never make it to seminary. You will never make it in the ministry. I am not allowing you to continue and want you to pack up your things and leave." Crushed, embarrassed, and confused, he had no idea what to do next.

Eventually, Bob began pastoring small congregations throughout New England that struggled to attract more educated ministers. The work was difficult and the salary low, but eventually Bob completed his undergraduate degree.

At this point in his story Bob addressed Dr. Cooper and me in front of the class.

"Dr. Cooper and Dr. Powers, I have been living with a great fear since arriving for this two-week intensive. The doctoral program requires a master of divinity as a prerequisite for admission. I never completed that degree. I've been waiting for one of you to tell me I don't belong and ask me to leave!"

Somehow communication had broken down and no one had delivered the life-altering news to the man.

"Bob," Dr. Cooper began, "The MDiv requirement has been waived due to your age and outstanding service to New England churches." Bob wept upon hearing the words. I wept, Dr. Cooper wept, as did every member of the class.

Bob became the informal chaplain of that cohort. His depth, wisdom, and humility drew classmates to him. He encouraged his fellow students to not give up in their doctoral studies, ministry settings, or thesis projects. Bob became an exemplar of redemptive influence for our class. God used Bob *because* of his crises, brokenness, and deep humility, *not* in spite of them. Bob continues to minister to pastors of small New England churches and their spouses.

> God used Bob *because* of his crises, brokenness, and deep humility, *not* in spite of them.

The Essential Foundations of the Redemptive Leadership Model

Here are the essential principles of the Redemptive Leadership Model:

- **Leadership is a developmental process occurring over the life span of a leader.** Each stage possesses a developmental task and the need to acquire key skills and experience. Each stage builds on the previous stage, incorporating past learnings but also qualitatively transcending it.

- **Pivotal transformation windows occur in the "crucible" experiences of our lives.** Often, the very strengths that produce outward success for a leader also create a crucible that reveals the leader's shadows, or dark side.

- **Counterintuitively, the crisis of this revelation opens a portal to an inward journey of transformation.** When engaged well, the process of brokenness and resulting humility reshapes the leader's heart.

- **Redemptive influence emerges as the leader discovers that deeper humility establishes a greater foundation of trust and the authority to speak into others' lives.** Paul's statement "In my weakness He is made strong" becomes real in the leader's life.

- **The ability to recognize the deeper redemptive narrative in others' lives allows the leader to support and guide individuals at key inflection points.** Redemptive leaders recognize pivotal moments, like Barnabas with John Mark, and discern the potential in the life of the individual obscured by the surface narrative. They then model, encourage, and mentor the leader in discovering and owning their own redemptive story.

- **The Redemptive Leadership Model is both linear and cyclic in nature.** As stated earlier, there is a linear progression from the competency stage through the redemption stage. It should be noted, however, that we cycle back through stages at different periods in our development. At times, we develop new competencies, new intelligences, etc. The potential for the deeper development of our hearts and redemptive influence continues throughout our lives as leaders.

- **Redemptive leadership must be understood as a framework, a mindset, and a value system.** Barnabas did not just "do" redemptive actions, he viewed the world and people through a redemptive lens. Guided by this framework he took action that seemed counterintuitive to others, including Paul. Obviously, Jesus repeatedly did likewise. The redemptive mindset, or operating system, permeates how redemptive leaders interpret the world.

The following graphic represents the five stages of the Redemptive Leadership Model. The far-left column maps the transition from externally focused influence (doing) to an internal focus on the leader's core (being). The far-right column describes the leader's shift from a primarily task-oriented focus to a focus on purpose and meaning. Thus, progressively through the transformation and redemption stages, influence emanates from the leader's core identity (heart).

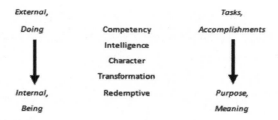

The Unusual Way I Came to Know Vernon Grounds

Dr. Vernon Grounds, now deceased, was a highly respected professor and leader at Denver Seminary where I am adjunct faculty. I never met Dr. Grounds personally, but I knew well his resume of accomplishment. He served as dean, president, professor emeritus, and eventually chancellor of Denver Seminary. He preached and lectured in hundreds of churches, colleges, universities, and seminaries across the United States, Europe, and Latin America. He authored multiple books and journal articles and contributed to many scholarly periodicals.

Dr. Grounds was a highly competent and accomplished man.

I came to know Dr. Grounds in a most unexpected manner—through the people he touched. Doug, an attorney and ministry leader, shared with me, "Entering seminary was a huge shift for me. It felt like a different universe from the practice of law. Seminary possessed a different vocabulary, mindset, and culture. Dr. Grounds met with me for lunch every other week. He guided, encouraged, and communicated his belief in me. I experienced our times together as very grounding."

Another leader shared that during a time of personal crisis "Dr. Grounds played a significant role in my life. He repeatedly invited me to meet on a park bench and brown bag our lunches. As we ate, we talked about life, our faith, and our hearts. Those times meant so much to me. I found it unbelievable that someone of his stature would invest so much time with me!"

On another occasion a leader told me, "One of the greatest influences in my life was Dr. Vernon Grounds. Early in my ministry journey he took me under his wing and stayed connected to me for decades. He walked with me through wonderful highs and through the lowest points in my adult life."

These spontaneously offered vignettes testify to the deep mark Dr. Grounds left in the lives of others. I am confident many others would tell similar stories of their encounters with him. Despite his accomplishments and the many demands on his schedule, he prioritized investing in people, often in their moments of difficulty. Dr. Vernon Grounds clearly left a legacy of redemptive influence by engaging others at critical moments. Like Barnabas, I don't know the shaping events in Dr. Grounds' life that created his sensitivity to others, but I am confident it arose from his own life journey.

My Purpose in Writing This Book

I wrote this book with three purposes in mind:

1. To stimulate a conversation about leadership beyond a competency framework. I suggest engaging those in your circle of peers to explore the deeper nature of leadership influence.

2. To spark curiosity regarding the theme of redemption in your personal story, particularly at your crisis and inflection points. As we recognize the deeper narrative of our story, we sensitize our ability to see the same in others.

3. To offer hope for emerging, re-emerging, and experienced leaders. *Emerging leaders*, expand your framework, or map, of your leadership journey. Embrace competency but guard against viewing it as the summit of your leadership growth. *Re-emerging leaders*, consider that your greatest impact

emerges because of your brokenness, not in spite of it. Experienced leaders, ignite the passion to recognize the deeper purpose and legacy of your leadership impact.

A Poem and a Prayer

Rainer Marie Rilke, in his poem "I Am Praying Again, Awesome One," concludes with this stanza addressing God:

Into them (God's hands) I place these fragments, my life,
And you God, spend them however you want.[2]

I offer this prayer for us all:

Father of light, in whom there is no darkness,
I pray for myself and my fellow travelers.
May the eyes of our hearts be opened
that we may experience the power of your redemption
in every recess of our lives.
May we view through your eyes the deeper narrative of
our story,
even at our well of Midian.
Grant that we may also recognize the deeper narrative
in others,
offering guidance and companionship like our brother,
Barnabas.
Allow us to carry the fresh scent of redemption to all
needing hope.
                                                            Amen.

Chapter 6 Reflection Questions

1. Reflect on the quote: "The Redemptive Leadership Model also views crisis and failure through a different optic. Instead of an ending, this model views them as a portal to go deeper." How does this concept apply to your life story? How does it apply to someone in your sphere of influence?

2. Why is humility an essential foundation to leadership influence? How does the importance of humility inform how you develop others?

3. Take a moment to review the section entitled "The Essential Foundations of the Redemptive Leadership Model." Consider journaling or discussing each bullet point and how it relates to your life. How would these observations impact the way you view leadership development in others?

4. What are your takeaways from this chapter and from the book as a whole?

NOTES

Chapter 2

1. Stephen R. Covey, *Principle-Centered Leadership* (New York: Simon & Schuster, 1991), 33–34.

2. Daniel Goleman, *Emotional Intelligence: Why It Can Matter More Than IQ*, 10th anniversary ed. (New York: Bantam Books, 2005).

3. "Martin Luther King Jr.—Biography," NobelPrize.Org, accessed September 3, 2018, https://www.nobelprize.org/prizes/peace/1964/king/biographical/.

4. "Martin Luther King Jr." *Wikipedia*, accessed August 26, 2018, https://en.wikipedia.org/w/index.php?title=Martin_Luther_King_Jr.&oldid=856557809.

5. "Letter From a Birmingham Jail." The Martin Luther King, Jr., Research and Education Institute, accessed September 3, 2018, https://kinginstitute.stanford.edu/king-papers/documents/letter-birmingham-jail.

6. Martin Luther King Jr., "'I Have a Dream,' Address Delivered at the March on Washington for Jobs and Freedom," The Martin Luther King, Jr., Research and Education Institute," King Institute Stanford, August 28, 1963, https://kinginstitute.stanford.edu/king-papers/documents/i-have-dream-address-delivered-march-washington-jobs-and-freedom.

7. "Jimmy Carter: Presidential Medal of Freedom Remarks on Presenting the Medal to Dr. Jonas E. Salk and to Martin

Luther King, Jr.," accessed September 3, 2018, http://www.
presidency.ucsb.edu/ws/?pid=7784.

Chapter 3

1. Bobby Clinton, "Listen Up Leaders!" Reprinted 1989,
    accessed September 3, 2018, http://bobbyclinton.com/store/
    clinton-gold/listen-up-leaders/.
2. Suzy Wetlaufer, "A Question of Character," *Harvard Business
    Review* (September–October 1999), https://hbr.org/1999/09/
    a-question-of-character.
3. Larry Donnithorne, *The West Point Way of Leadership* (New
    York: Currency Doubleday, 1993).
4. Fred Kiel, *Return on Character: The Real Reason Leaders and
    Their Companies Win* (Boston: Harvard Business Review
    Press, 2015).
5. "Baron Thomas Babington Macauley Quotes," Quot.dog,
    accessed September 3, 2018, https://quot.dog/quotes/the-
    measure-of-a-man-s-character-is-what-he-would-do-if-he-
    knew-he-never-would-be-found-out.
6. "Character Is Like a Tree and Reputation Like a ShadowThe
    Shadow Is What We Think of It and the Tree Is the Real
    Thing," ReputationXL.com, February 20, 2015, http://
    www.reputationxl.com/quotes/character-is-like-a-tree-and-
    reputation-like-a-shadow-the-shadow-is-what-we-think-of-
    it-and-the-tree-is-the-real-thing/.
7. "Mark Twain Quotations – Moon," TwainQuotes.com,
    accessed September 9, 2018, www.twainquotes.com/Moon.
    html.
8. "Helen Keller Quotes," BrainyQuote.com, accessed
    September 3, 2018, https://www.brainyquote.com/quotes/
    helen_keller_101340.

9. "Al Gore – Nobel Lecture," NobelPrize.org, accessed September 3, 2018, https://www.nobelprize.org/prizes/peace/2007/gore/26118-al-gore-nobel-lecture-2007/.

10. "John F. Kennedy Quotations," John F. Kennedy Presidential Library and Museum, jfklibrary.org, accessed September 3, 2018, https://www.jfklibrary.org/Research/Research-Aids/Ready-Reference/JFK-Quotations.aspx#C.

Chapter 4

1. "Metamorphoo," Gerhard Kittel, Gerhard Friedrich, and Geoffrey William Bromiley, eds., *Theological Dictionary of the New Testament* (Grand Rapids, MI: William B. Eerdmans, 1985).

2. "Anakalypto," Gerhard Kittel, Gerhard Friedrich, and Geoffrey William Bromiley, eds., *Theological Dictionary of the New Testament* (Grand Rapids, MI: William B. Eerdmans, 1985).

3. "Hypomone," Henry George Liddell and Robert Scott, eds., *Lexicon Abridged from Liddell and Scott's Greek-English Lexicon* (Charleston, SC: Nabu Press, 2010).

4. Henri J.M. Nouwen, *In the Name of Jesus: Reflections on Christian Leadership with Study Guide for Groups and Individuals* (New York: Crossroad Publishing, 2002).

Chapter 5

1. *Les Miserables*, directed by Bille August (Sony Pictures Home Entertainment, 1998).

2. "Mary Johnson and Oshea Israel," StoryCorps.com, accessed September 3, 2018, https://storycorps.org/listen/mary-johnson-and-oshea-israel/.

3. "Apolytrosis," Gerhard Kittel, Gerhard Friedrich, and Geoffrey William Bromiley, eds., *Theological Dictionary of the*

New Testament (Grand Rapids, MI: William B. Eerdmans, 1985).

4.   "Randy Alcorn Quotations – A Quote from *Heaven*," Goodreads.com, accessed September 10, 2018, https://www. goodreads.com/quotes/606066-jesus-miracles-provide-us-with-a-sample-of-the-meaning.

5.   David Brooks, *The Road to Character* (New York: Random House, 2016), loc. 92 of 5695, Kindle.

6.   Ibid.

7.   David Brooks, *The Road to Character* (New York: Random House, 2016), loc. 156 of 5695, Kindle.

Chapter 6

1.   "The Journey" © Many Rivers Press. Printed with permission from Many Rivers Press, www.davidwhyte.com, from The House of Belonging (Langley, WA: Many Rivers Press, 1997).

2.   *Rilke's Book of Hours: Love Poems to God* by Rainer Maria Rilke (1900), translated by Anita Barrows and Joanna Macy (New York: Riverhead Books, 1997), 137.